Bad Advice

Bad Advice

a nasty little book for good girls who want to be bad

Martha Vialli

with

Karen Krizanovich

Roadside Amusements
an imprint of
Chamberlain Bros.
a member of Penguin Group (USA) Inc.
New York

ROADSIDE AMUSEMENTS
an imprint of
CHAMBERLAIN BROS.
Published by the Penguin Group
Penguin Group (USA) Inc., 375 Hudson Street, New York, New York 10014, USA
Penguin Group (Canada), 90 Eglinton Avenue East, Suite 700, Toronto, Ontario
M4P 2Y3, Canada (a division of Pearson Penguin Canada Inc.)
Penguin Books Ltd, 80 Strand, London WC2R 0RL, England
Penguin Ireland, 25 St Stephen's Green, Dublin 2, Ireland
(a division of Penguin Books Ltd)
Penguin Group (Australia), 250 Camberwell Road, Camberwell, Victoria 3124,
Australia (a division of Pearson Australia Group Pty Ltd)
Penguin Books India Pvt Ltd, 11 Community Centre, Panchsheel Park,
New Delhi–110 017, India
Penguin Group (NZ), Cnr Airborne and Rosedale Roads, Albany, Auckland 1310,
New Zealand (a division of Pearson New Zealand Ltd)
Penguin Books (South Africa) (Pty) Ltd, 24 Sturdee Avenue, Rosebank,
Johannesburg 2196, South Africa

Penguin Books Ltd, Registered Offices: 80 Strand, London WC2R 0RL, England

Published simultaneously in Canada

Produced by Essential Works Ltd.
168a Camden Street, London NW1 9PT, England
Text: Karen Krizanovich
Illustrations: Leonie O'Moore
Design: Kate Ward and Barbara Doherty

An application has been submitted to register this book
with the Library of Congress.

ISBN 1-59609-088-X

Printed in the United States of America
1 3 5 7 9 10 8 6 4 2

For my parents, John and Eve, and my husband, David,
who love me no matter how bad I am. Right?

Introduction

Darlings,

What is the world coming to? There is just too much goodness and too many fine intentions swimming around the great Western gene pool for my liking. One of my favorite T-shirts bears the image of a very nice and compact 9mm Glock automatic pistol, and above it the legend, "New York—it ain't Kansas." Yet as anyone who has recently been in the once mighty Gotham will tell you, it might as well be Dorothy's home state. Everyone seems so well behaved and polite, it makes me want to puke. Which I do, often enough, and to great effect. Although not in Times Square, of course, because that would just get me arrested.

Darlings, in desperation at how we women of the world seem to be losing our hard-won feminine right to be demanding, ornery, contrary, and downright difficult, I have engaged the help of my longtime friend Karen Krizanovich (she wisely moved to London absolutely ages ago, which is why we're still pals) and decided to hand out all the wonderful and truly BAD advice that you'll find between the pages of this lovely daily planner. She might have written it all down, but of course it's all my idea. Oh, and Karen, honey? America is still too small for the two of us.

I've been asked by the publisher to point out that if you choose to follow any of the advice as prescribed in this book, then bad things may well happen to you. Or other people, because of you. Of course they're men, so they don't understand, the poor dears, but that is the whole point of this book. Anyway, whatever, don't try this at home and if you do, don't blame me or Karen or the publisher because we won't get you out of jail or pay your fines or hospital bills.

But enjoy the book as best you can and remember, act like a real woman should—badly.

Love, Martha Vialli

Get Back Together with Your Boyfriend

....

You will need: to make your eyes water

....

After breakfast in bed with last night's conquest (see Day 365), go home wearing one of his shirts. Shower and call your boyfriend in tears. Accuse him of being with someone else last night. Tell him that you think it's all over even though you love him so much. Hang up and pull the line out of the wall. When he storms over to your place, answer the door wearing nothing but (if you're feeling really bad) that shirt.

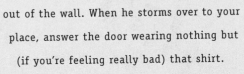

♥♥♥ ROMANCE ♥♥♥

Flirt Successfully

....

You will need: a desirable man and no shame

....

Identify your target. Never mind if he is wearing a wedding band or is with his kids. Smoothly and imperceptibly glide over near him and strike up a conversation. Interrupt if you must. At this point, spill your drink all over him or faint. Whatever you do, it must be something that ensures contact between you and him. When the moment is right, ask him out. If he says no, ask to have a drink with him.

If he still says no, burst into tears.

Works every time.

♥♥♥ ROMANCE ♥♥♥

Have a Quiet Day

You will need: eye drops and a soft place to land

Whenever anyone tries to tell you anything, quickly turn away. Apply pupil-dilating eye drops (which will also act as tears), wail, then fling yourself onto the soft place, screaming, "No! No! No! I can't bear it!" Soon the whole office, if not the whole town, will be shaking in its boots. You won't be bothered and your prescription will always be ready at the pharmacy.

Be Naive

You will need: false eyelashes

Being bad has its drawbacks. Sometimes you have to look as if you wouldn't hurt a fly. Of course you wouldn't hurt a fly, although you may take its boyfriend, job, and inheritance. Buy the biggest, fluffiest false eyelashes you can find. Wear them into the office. Look sweet. Bat your doe eyes at all and sundry. Your attitude should be that of Audrey Hepburn surrounded by a roomful of puppies. Then go in for the kill.

●●● OFFICE ●●●

GET THREE PAIRS OF SHOES FOR THE PRICE OF ONE

. . . .

You will need: a shoe store where you will never shop again

. . . .

Buy a pair of shoes and fit the soles with carpeting. Wear them for a brief while. Take them back and say they didn't match your dress after all. Take that other pair; do the same with those. Make sure that the last person who waited on you isn't there, pick the most beautiful pair of shoes in the shop, and exchange for them. If the clerk says no, promise to never come back again if you get them. Works every time.

☼ ☼ ☼ LEISURE ☼ ☼ ☼

GET LOTS OF ATTENTION

· ·

You will need: a turban and a caftan

· ·

Buy a matching turban and caftan. Sling on large items of jewelry, long false nails, and eyelashes. Swan into your local shop and start handling the merchandise, saying things like, "Darling, my dear old aunt had one of these and they were DIVINE." Bump a few other shoppers out of the way on purpose and butt into line just to make your point.

☼ ☼ ☼ LEISURE ☼ ☼ ☼

Be Lucky

....

You will need: a big bag of lies

....

There is no such thing as bad luck. It's all a matter of how you look at it. A flat tire is a new way to look weak and helpless and perhaps to meet a knight in shining armor (with a wrench and a jack). Your boyfriend hasn't left you—you both drifted apart because he couldn't take your quest to acquire the world's largest collection of mascara. Lie to everyone and you'll be incredibly lucky.

❀ ❀ ❀   ETIQUETTE   ❀ ❀ ❀

Insult an Old Person

....

You will need: the guise of being helpful

....

Carry a package for an older person, preferably a woman. As you hand the package back, exclaim, "My, what luxurious hair you have on your arms. Are you from Hairy Island?" or "Maybe you should buy helium from now on— I may not be here to help you all the time." Then depart quickly, calling a taxi to drown out any parting remarks from your victim.

❀ ❀ ❀ ETIQUETTE ❀ ❀ ❀

Win Over the Board Meeting

You will need: inside information on all board participants

Give your presentation, being as professional as possible, but pepper your delivery with not-so-subtle hints. "The projections for next quarter are likely to rise as SOMEONE HERE IS GETTING DIVORCED BECAUSE HIS WIFE KNOWS ABOUT HIS SHODDY AFFAIR." You can be subtler if you must. The board will fear you and accept all your ideas.

●●● OFFICE ●●●

Day 10

Stake Your Territory

You will need: a fast walking stride
and a great manicure

Spot your victim. Let your eyes sweep around the
office, then walk as quickly as you can to your
mark. Get too close. Slide your perfect nails
under their lapels and say, "Oh, I'm so sorry.
This is such a beautiful jacket, I couldn't help
myself. You have excellent taste." Hang on their
every word as they stare into your eyes and then
tell him to get lost. They won't dare to cross you.

● ● ● OFFICE ● ● ●

Day 11

Baffle Your Boyfriend

....

You will need: a mind and a
cell-phone alarm

....

Set the cell alarm to vibrate and to go off in your pocket
every 10 minutes. During a romantic dinner or
a quiet night in, when a conversation starts between
you and your loved one, whenever the alarm goes off
(which of course he cannot hear), completely change
conversational tack. If you were praising his family, turn
on them. If you were against taking cruises, be wildly
in favor of them. If you were moving toward a night
of raw passion, turn tepid.

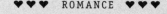 ♥♥♥ ROMANCE ♥♥♥

Be Miss Right

....

You will need: to suppress virtually all of
your personality

....

Men want one thing, which can be described in two words:
"easy life." Find your victim, er, man, and be what he wants
you to be. That usually involves hanging on his every word
("I'm dying to hear what that guy at the auto part place
said . . ."), making him feel like a winner no matter what
he does ("No one can ball up a tissue and almost get it in
the basket like you, Bill!"), and shutting up and smiling a
lot. Make him feel admired by a silent, adoring mystery girl
and you'll soon have him in your clutches.

♥ ♥ ♥   ROMANCE   ♥ ♥ ♥

INSULT A YOUNG PERSON

....

You will need: knowledge that they won't be your boss in years to come

....

Take advantage of youth's propensity for politeness and deference by making yourself feel good at their expense. To a cherub-faced teen say, "Ah, puppy fat will melt away as you grow up. It's the bitch fat you should worry about." To a makeup-slathered girl say, "Do you work at the circus? Oh, no, of course. They REMOVE their makeup there, silly me."

❀ ❀ ❀ ETIQUETTE ❀ ❀ ❀

FIX A FRIENDSHIP

. . . .

You will need: a big slice of humble pie

. . . .

Call your friend until she picks up the phone or
raises the restraining order. Ask her to be your guest
at her favorite restaurant. Take her there and
apologize endlessly for being a bitch and alienating
her. Tell her you were diagnosed with a temporary
but virulent mental illness that made you a
sociopath—but, happily, you are all cured now and
really want her forgiveness and value her friendship.
If she won't be your friend, steal her pet. If
she won't be your friend, she won't
have one either.

❀ ❀ ❀ ETIQUETTE ❀ ❀ ❀

Day 15

SHOW MOM YOU'RE A GREAT COOK

....

You will need: a huge freezer, aluminum foil, dated labels, some raw food, Band-Aids, and garbage

....

Buy as much frozen, expensive, and delicious preprepared food as you can. Take it out of its identifying wrapper. Place it in foil and put a recent or future date on it in your handwriting. Invite Mom over for dinner. Make a big deal out of it: "It's just some leftovers I froze!" as you trot out Duck à l'Orange, Beef Wellington, and Baked Alaska. Add some "homemade" touches—slightly raw veggies, a touch too much pepper, etc., to the preprepared food.

☺ ☺ ☹ FAMILY ☺ ☺ ☹

Day 16

TORMENT YOUR
EX-SMOKER DAD

. . . .

You will need: cartons of cigarettes, full
ashtrays, and stress

. . . .

Ask your ex-smoker dad to step into the "smoking area."
Tell him you have some very bad news to relay, then beat
around the bush. Play with an open pack of cigarettes.
Light one up. Let it sit unsmoked in the ashtray. Light
another one, waving your arms around and saying how you
are having such trouble even telling him the bad news.
Watch him crack.

☺ ☺ ☹ FAMILY ☺ ☺ ☹

Get a Free Bodyguard

....

You will need: a few weeks at a gym and skimpy clothing

....

Put on your skimpy clothes and go to the gym. Hang around the free weights and look helpless. Find a large, burly man who has no friends and flirt outrageously. Get his number. Stop going to the gym. When you next need a bodyguard, call your burly man up and ask him out, telling him to wear a suit. Give him an earpiece to wear and tell him your dangerous ex may be lurking anywhere.

☼ ☼ ☼ LEISURE ☼ ☼ ☼

Be Fabulous

....

You will need: one perfect outfit and
a loud mouth

....

Look fantastic—not one hair out of place—and
waltz into a room. Spread your arms wide and cry
out a woman's name. When everyone is looking say,
"Marsha! Darling!" and run into the next room. Make
a big fuss. "This carpeting is fantastic! Where'd you
get it?!" You can even drink too much and throw food
on the floor, because when you are well-dressed
and positive, you CAN.

☼ ☼ ☼ LEISURE ☼ ☼ ☼

Get a Raise

You will need: a file full of work and a
small puppy

Come into your boss's office with your arms full of work files and a puppy. Ask to sit down. Say, "I've proven myself to you and this company," shaking the files a bit, "and I would like a raise, especially now that I have another mouth to feed." If your boss denies you or says, "Let's discuss this when you've worked for us longer than a month," mention that you know he dresses as a woman and that you know where he can find the right size evening shoes.

OFFICE

Get a Better Office

You will need: a doctor's letter (or a pal
who can write like a doctor)

Get your "doctor" to write a letter saying that you have muraphobia—a fear of walls—and therefore must have an office with no fewer than three sides of glass looking out onto a panoramic view of either city or river. Have your doctor add that if you don't get this particular office setup, your illness can result in unpredictable projectile vomiting and/or uncontrollable sobbing.

●●● OFFICE ●●●

Give a Dose of Dandruff

....

You will need: oatmeal and a blender

....

Put a cup of oatmeal into a blender and run until fine.
Put a small amount into a spice shaker and keep this
in your handbag. Whenever you spy your enemy sitting
down, walk past and shake some fine oatmeal onto
their shoulders and into their hair.

💣 💣 💣 MISCHIEF 💣 💣 💣

Ruin a Friendship

....

You will need: to tell the truth

....

Take a friend aside and tell her that she's gaining a little weight. Maybe she should get her eyes done? Has she ever considered finishing school? And you'd be happy to go with her to buy a wig. Basically, tell her the truth about herself and she will never speak to you again.

🔥 🔥 🔥 🔥 MISCHIEF 🔥 🔥 🔥 🔥

Look Great Naked

. . . .

You will need: a movement-sensitive
dimmer switch

. . . .

Install the dimmer switch. Plop your date on the sofa or
bed and begin to dance a striptease. With ease, remove
your clothes (which are many). The dimmer switch should
slowly, imperceptibly take the lights down lower and lower.
The room will be inky darkness by the time your
enormous panties hit the floor.

♥♥♥   ROMANCE   ♥♥♥

Be a Great Lover

....

You will need: tons of energy and enthusiasm
no matter what

....

Sex is like dancing: harder than it looks and hard not to
lead. To be a great lover, you must be eager for everything
your lover presents no matter how boring or painful, and
make them feel loved, in charge, and desired but not in a
sex-toy kind of way. When they touch you, make
murmuring noises such as, "Oh, that feels wonderful," even
if you can't feel anything. Do not ask if they are done yet.

♥♥♥ ROMANCE ♥♥♥

Trip Up Your Office Enemy

You will need: a few yards of fishing line on a fast-retrieve reel

Watch the pathway where your office enemy goes regularly. Get their schedule; especially note when they are carrying a cup of coffee or that ugly, gross soy drink they consume. Place the hook of the fishing line onto a low, solid point guaranteed to catch their ankles in one go. As they fall onto their soy drink, snatch the line back and slip it into your bag. Go to help them up and fall on them.

● ● ● OFFICE ● ● ●

Get a Key to the Executive Bathroom

You will need: to become friends with a janitor

Stay late and meet the nighttime janitor. Pass on almost finished perfumes to any of them, become their friend, and then ask them for the universal key to the executive bathroom. Have that key copied. Watch who goes there, and when. If caught in there, say you'd lost a diamond earring while you were having sex with one of the visiting executives who asked you to marry him at the last big party.

● ● ● OFFICE ● ● ●

Be Witty

....

You will need: a few choice lines from *What Ever Happened to Baby Jane?* (Do not use Oscar Wilde or Dorothy Parker: too obvious.)

....

Memorize bits of script or text. The next time there is a lull in conversation or whenever someone says something funny, throw in, "But you are, Blanche, you are in that chair!" or "Well, cheer up, Mary; living alone has its compensations. Heaven knows it's marvelous being able to spread out in bed like a swastika." No one need know they're not original. Even David Letterman has scriptwriters.

💣 💣 💣 MISCHIEF 💣 💣 💣

Tell Someone the Ugly Truth (and get away with it)

....

You will need: a straight face

....

Tell someone the truth that you've been holding in for so long ("You're so ugly! Is that your real face?" "Do you HAVE a dentist?"). After a day or two, apologize. "I just want to say that I am really, really sorry. How could I do that to you? You're a kind, thoughtful person. I hate myself. Do you accept my apology? It's important that I know. I can't stand it any longer!" Burst into tears. Run to the bathroom. Laugh like a hyena.

HAVE A PERSONAL SLAVE

. . . .

You will need: someone with low self-esteem
and a lot of time on their hands

. . . .

Befriend a loser. Go shopping with them and buy them
an outfit that sort of looks like a uniform. Invite them
over to your next party and ask them to help out with
the drinks and food. Then ask them to help with the
cleaning up and the garbage. Thank them and let them
take home the remainder of the caramelized Bugles
leftover from the party.

☼ ☼ ☼ LEISURE ☼ ☼ ☼

"COMFORT" A DUMPED FRIEND

. . . .

You will need: a box of tissues and chocolates

. . . .

Rush over to your dumped friend's house—she'll be in tears. "There there," you say, "he just didn't love you! Good riddance! There are plenty more fish in the sea. Besides"—you grab a tissue and dab your eyes—"he was terrible in bed." Offer her chocolates: make sure she eats several while you say, "Now you have to lose weight because you're back on the market!"

☼ ☼ ☼ LEISURE ☼ ☼ ☼

Be a Hacker (or look just like one)

You will need: badly fitted jeans, a knitted wool hat, poor posture, and a cup full of jargon

Befriend an IT insider at work and get everyone's passwords. Jam the system by changing their passwords. Within moments, change into your hacker ensemble and wave your arms saying, "I can fix this mess! Stand back!" Sit down and reinstall all passwords. You should get a raise and new respect from everyone (except IT).

●●● OFFICE ●●●

Brag Yourself Up

You will need: a small trinket with which to play

During a chat with coworkers, idly mention that you saw an e-mail from the boss. It was full of praise for work recently done and promised a raise to those responsible. "Didn't you get one?" you ask with a straight, innocent face. When the rest of your office buddies shake their heads, fiddle with your trinket and say, "Oh. Sorry."

Baffle Your Pals

. . . .

You will need: people to impress, illegible notes, and a cell phone

. . . .

Gather a group of friends on the pretext that you have something to tell them. When assembled, ask if there are any questions. Ignore everyone. Call a guy Shirley and then answer your cell. Stare for a long time at your "notes," then write something illegibly on a pad and show everyone. Answer your phone again and then rush off. Return home with gifts for everyone. Now they'll listen to anything you have to say.

☼ ☼ ☼ LEISURE ☼ ☼ ☼

Change a Tire

. . . .

You will need: a bikini and a car with
a flat tire

. . . .

The minute you hear the *thump-thump-thump* of a flat
tire, pull over. Out of the glove box, take your bikini
and put it on. Step outside the car and go look at the
tire, leaning over and sticking out your backside.
Several cars should have pulled up with male offers
of help within seconds. If women pull up, they
will offer you a blanket.

✵ ✵ ✵ LEISURE ✵ ✵ ✵

Day 35

MAKE YOUR MOTHER PROUD

You will need: total obedience and not a shred of pride

Wear the most
repulsive item of clothing given to
you by your mother. Put your hair in a do she
would admire. Buy a bouquet of her favorite flowers
(or candy or rump roast). Wear shoes she would like
and her style of makeup. Come to see her and agree
with everything she says. After one hour, excuse
yourself politely. Go outside. Scream. Repeat.

☺ ☺ ☹ FAMILY ☺ ☺ ☹

HANDLE A MOTHER-IN-LAW

You will need: acting skills

Praise your mother-in-law's cooking. Make a big fuss about how delicious everything is. After dinner, get terrible stomach cramps and beg to be taken home. Intimate the next day that the doctor said it was food poisoning but that you wouldn't hear a word of it. Besides, no one else was poisoned. Hint that you know she'd poisoned your food only.

☺ ☺ ☹ FAMILY ☺ ☺ ☹

GET OUT OF TIPPING

. . . .

You will need: the ability to get hysterical

. . . .

Go into an eatery with a friend. Pay the bill without adding the tip. Get noticeably upset with the waiter. Murmur incoherently. Scream and run out of the restaurant. Have your friend explain that you were scared by a waitress and/or a waiter as a child and your doctor advised you never to tip, lest you suffer flashbacks.

☼ ☼ ☼ LEISURE ☼ ☼ ☼

BE A CAR "EXPERT"

. . . .

You will need: the names of a few car parts

. . . .

Start a conversation with guys about cars. Then jump in with any jargon you can muster. "My brother once had a fender blowout," you say. "Luckily, he had a dipstick and was able to fix it." If anyone laughs, use terms such as heel-and-toeing and double-declutching since no one knows what they mean.

☼ ☼ ☼ LEISURE ☼ ☼ ☼

Make Mantrap Gravy

....

You will need: the ruined pan in which you
burned the roast

....

If anything can bring the word marriage to a man's lips,
it's gravy. Take your pan and put it on the stove-top. Heat
until bubbling. Throw in some water and flour, and stir. If
lumpy, curse. Use a whisk and smooth until the
consistency of gravy. Add salt and pepper. Ladle generously
over burned beef, raw potatoes, or, in fact, cardboard.
Serve. Expect a proposal. Decline, of course.

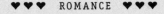

♥ ♥ ♥   ROMANCE   ♥ ♥ ♥

Break Up a Man and His Best Friend

. . . .

You will need: a man with a best friend

. . . .

Get a man to fall in love with you. As he becomes more and more enamored, start to compare him to his best friend. "David's so kind," you say. "Not like you. And he's so sweet. Not like you. And he's so handsome. Not like you. And he's so polite. Not like you." Carry on in this vein until the vein on his forehead stands out.

❤ ❤ ❤ ROMANCE ❤ ❤ ❤

Get a Rake-Off for a Floor Model

....

You will need: anything you want that is on display in a shop

....

Find something on display and ask the clerk if you can buy the floor model. Act as if there is something "wrong" with you. Mid-discussion, slightly scratch or damage it. Exclaim, "Oh. It's damaged." Give the clerks who have now gathered around a wild look. Say, "May I have this one, please?" Hope security doesn't arrive.

☼ ☼ ☼ LEISURE ☼ ☼ ☼

Get Free Makeup

. . . .

You will need: a professional makeup
artist who specializes in prosthetics

. . . .

Buy one cheap item of makeup. Create a fake rash
where the makeup would be applied. Go back to the
counter, show them the rash, and ask for another
kind of product. Try that and have your artist make
a large boil on your neck. Go back and say, "I've never
had this problem before. Are you sure that your
makeup isn't tainted?" If you have selected a new
or particularly nervous clerk, you can get a bagful.

☼ ☼ ☼ LEISURE ☼ ☼ ☼

Write a Best Seller

....

You will need: dirt on an agent or publisher

....

Hire a private detective to get sensitive information on the publisher or agent of your choice. Make sure it is juicy, hot, dangerous information that would ruin them if it ever hit the papers. Write a book about framing a publisher/agent—changing the names, of course— and know it will get the marketing it deserves to become a big hit. Or else.

🖤 🖤 🖤 MISCHIEF 🖤 🖤 🖤

Get That Apartment for Less!

· ·

You will need: some shrimp or maybe
a mackerel

· ·

Find an apartment you like. Visit it one more time
with a friend who can distract the real-estate agent
while you surreptitiously nail a mackerel into a closet
or stuff a shrimp down a hollow curtain rod. The smell
will not only encourage the seller to drop the price but
will also put off competitive buyers.

🕭 🕭 🕭 MISCHIEF 🕭 🕭 🕭

Find Out if He Really Loves You

. . . .

You will need: a Mexican restaurant
and farting skill

. . . .

As a romantic treat, take your lover to dinner at a Mexican
restaurant and on to a Swedish movie. Load up on the
beans and beer. Sit through the movie cuddling, squirming,
and breaking wind. If he loves you he'll still
want to worship at the altar of your
loveliness, under the covers, that night.

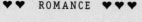

♥♥♥   ROMANCE   ♥♥♥

Deal with Being in Love

....

You will need: a good hard slap

....

If you're sending flowers, feeling dreamy all day long, and waiting for that special someone to call, there's a good chance you're in love. Unless you are sending flowers to yourself, dreamily staring into a mirror, or waiting for your answering service to tell you that you've just called, you're in deep trouble. Snap out of it. Get a close friend to slap you. Hard.

♥ ♥ ♥ ROMANCE ♥ ♥ ♥

Get a Favor from the Office Bore

You will need: eyes painted
on your eyelids

Lean on the bore's desk. Make sure he's paying
attention. Ask him for his advice about something
obscure—the theremin, the genesis of *Star Trek*,
character design of the *X-Men*, anything—and
pretend to listen. Close your eyes (he will think you
are still listening intently). As he reaches the end
of his knowledge (this will be some four
hours later), ask your favor. It will be granted.

● ● ● OFFICE ● ● ●

Have Whiter Work Teeth

You will need: blue lipstick, strong coffee, blueberries, licorice, tea

Give out a batch of blue-ish lipstick to all your coworkers. Tell them it will make everyone look younger. Supply everyone with extra-strong coffee. Put out blueberries and licorice on snack dishes. Give non-coffee drinkers strong tea. You drink nothing but spring water and don't smoke. After a few weeks your teeth will look whiter than anyone else's—in the office, at least.

☛ ☛ ☛ OFFICE ☚ ☚ ☚

ALIENATE YOUR SISTER

························

You will need: a sister, preferably your own

························

Go to lunch with your sister and tell her that you've been

harboring a terrible secret for years and that you can bear

it no longer. Tell her that your parents never liked her and

favored you all the time. This put a terrible burden on you.

Tell her that your father isn't sure she's his and your

mother isn't sure she's hers. Then tell her you slept

with her partner. Let her pay for lunch.

☺ ☺ ☹ FAMILY ☺ ☺ ☹

Day 50

IMPROVE YOUR MEMORY

. . . .

You will need: your family and some
uncomfortable questions

. . . .

Invite your family over for a big slap-up meal. Right in the
middle, while everyone is chowing down, ask your father,
"Dad, who is Uncle Fred? He came over to see Mom a lot
when you weren't around—isn't that right, Mom?" Ask
your siblings if they returned the money they stole from
the family coffers or if your little brother ever did
admit to denting the car.

☺ 😐 ☹ FAMILY ☺ 😐 ☹

Play Rough

· ·

You will need: someone whom you
dislike intensely

· ·

If the person you dislike starts to give you trouble say,
"It's not my fault that you can't hold a relationship
together with a piece of string. Just kidding!" If they
wince but persist, add, "I can't help it that you made
those bad investments. Just kidding." If they still
won't leave you alone, attack for the final time by
saying, "It's not my fault your mother didn't love
you." Don't add the "just kidding" part.

❀ ❀ ❀ ETIQUETTE ❀ ❀ ❀

Fire Your Cleaner/ Trainer/Chef without Paying Compensation

· ·

You will need: impossible demands

· ·

Don't tell them you can't afford them—just ask them to do the impossible. Any true professional will have their limits. It is up to you to find and exceed them. Ask your personal trainer for a massage; ask your cleaner to wash the dirt outside; make your chef talk to the vegetables.

❀ ❀ ❀ ETIQUETTE ❀ ❀ ❀

MEET AND DRINK WITH CELEBRITIES

. . . .

You will need: an eye for famous faces, one good outfit

. . . .

Go to a bar or club where famous people regularly go. Become friendly with the staff. Find out who will be there whenever. Come in on that night and hang around. When you spy your famous person, push through the bar crowd and pretend to get a drink. Sidle over to the famous person and bend over so your bottom touches them. You'll both say, "Oh! Sorry!" and there you have it.

☼ ☼ ☼ LEISURE ☼ ☼ ☼

TEACH SOMEONE WHEN TO QUIT

You will need: a tearful eye

First choose your target. A guy who has been smiling at you inanely on the street, preferably. Go up to him, clutching your eye, and ask him if he can help. There's "something" in your eye. Spend at least thirty minutes with him attempting to help you without letting him actually touch you or your eye. Keep saying, "It's still there!" until he gives up. Now he knows when to quit.

☼ ☼ ☼ LEISURE ☼ ☼ ☼

Have a Nasty Affair

· ·

You will need: someone you like

· ·

Find your person with whom to have wild, passionate, and dirty adult times. Have them meet you in broom closets, alleys, parks, or parked cars—anywhere degrading, dirty, and humiliating. After weeks of this behavior, he will ask you, "When can we use a regular bed?" You reply, "I can't believe you said that!" and never see him again.

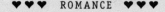 ♥♥♥ ROMANCE ♥♥♥

Get Rid Of an Admirer

....

You will need: an hour for a free makeover

....

Got an admirer who loves you for you? Go to your favorite beauty counter and book yourself in for a makeover. Tell them you want radical, cutting-edge makeup. Call your admirer and invite him to meet you at your local supermarket. Between the makeover and the supermarket flourescent lighting, the man would have to be off balance not to leave you alone for good.

If he doesn't, he's a stalker.

♥♥♥　ROMANCE　♥♥♥

MAKE THAT CALL YOU'VE BEEN AVOIDING

....

You will need: a cell phone and a very
noisy room

....

Make that call on your cell phone. Make sure the
room is noisy enough. When the person you've been
dreading speaking to answers, say what you have to
say. Wait for them to speak. Tell them, "I can't hear
you, but I hope you agree with what I said. I'll take
that as a yes." Then cut them off.

❀ ❀ ❀ ETIQUETTE ❀ ❀ ❀

DEAL WITH UGLY BABIES

....

You will need: good hard liquor in a hip flask (and running shoes)

....

When presented with a truly troll-like baby, sneak a sip from your handy flask and exclaim, "My! What a lovely shawl!" or "Who took the photo? It's amazing!" or, after the liquor has kicked in, "Awww! Doesn't he look like a baby wildebeest?" N.B. You may need those running shoes now.

❀ ❀ ❀ ETIQUETTE ❀ ❀ ❀

Maximize Your Return from the Gym

. . . .

You will need: workout clothes, hair gel, blush, a spray bottle of water, heart monitor

. . . .

Get into your workout gear. Slick your hair back and toss on some blush. Spray the front, back, and armpits of your T-shirt plus your face with the water. Run into your home or office sighing, "Oh, heavens. What a run (or workout, etc). Just didn't have time to shower."

☼ ☼ ☼ LEISURE ☼ ☼ ☼

Day 60

Look Like You Can Cook

You will need: flour and many messy pans

Sprinkle food in some pans and throw them into the oven. Let them cook for an hour or so. Take out and arrange in a scary mess around the oven and countertop. Put on your favorite gown and streak it with flour. Put some in your hair, too. Stay this way until guests arrive. Complain about the mess you made, then say, "Ah, but what wouldn't I do for my friends? It's all worth it. Even the blood."

Help the Opposition

You will need: enough clout to
call a meeting

Whenever your office rival has an idea, suggest a meeting to discuss it. Make them scramble to deliver the idea, then shoot it down with everything you can think of—even cheap shots will work. "That's a sensible idea," you say, "seeing as it will only cost thousands of human resource hours and quite a bit of cash. Also, it just isn't aesthetic." Remember, the situation is on your side: meetings are the effective way to ruin any great idea.

Avoid the Dirty Work

You will need: the ability to be truly mediocre

Write a report without verbs or fail to understand the new computer; let the office coffee pot bedazzle you or show everyone that you don't know the difference between spoiled and good milk. This will not only show people that you can't possibly do these little jobs, they may well delegate less work to you in the future.

Be That Mysterious Girl

....

You will need: something to occupy your
mind for a long time, i.e., a symphony
in composition

....

Engage a man in "conversation." He'll either want to talk
about himself—or not talk at all. Handle it by having
something to think about—composing music, designing
a museum, practicing your symbolic logic. That way, when
he asks you, "Have you any unexpressed
thoughts?" you can just
smile enigmatically.

♥ ♥ ♥   ROMANCE   ♥ ♥ ♥

Be Lauren Bacall
for the Day

....

You will need: a few sharp witticisms, great
hair, a good pout, and matte red lipstick

....

An extension of the Mysterious Girl ploy is the Lauren
Bacall ploy. Grow a glossy curtain of hair under which
you can hide if you like. Outline your lips in Hollywood
matte red and be ready to throw a few punches verbally.
Good universal ones are: "I feel so dirty now" and
"I like that in a man."

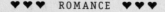 ROMANCE

Ruin an Enemy's Looks

....

You will need: a trophy, scissors, and a sheet

....

No acid needed here! Offer your enemy a peace pipe of a
haircut. Tell her that you've finished beauty school,
graduating at the top of your class. You even won an
award for best haircutter (gesture toward the trophy).
To mend the fences, offer to cut her hair for free.
Throw a sheet over her shoulders and start cutting.
You'll only need to do this once.

🏴 🏴 🏴 **MISCHIEF** 🏴 🏴 🏴

Be an Heiress (fallen on hard times)

· ·

You will need: a bit of Scotch tape

· · · · · · · · · · · · · · · · · · · ·

Wear vintage clothing, slip the odd foreign word into your speech, and wear a peculiar brooch. Take some Scotch tape and fold it in half to make it a circle that is sticky on both sides. Say, "Do you know that my family invented this? Unfortunately, Great Uncle Roger lost our inventor's fortune, but I still get a small income from every bit of tape that is folded." N.B. Do not substitute Post-it notes for tape—that's from a movie.

💣 💣 💣 MISCHIEF 💣 💣 💣

Arouse Your Boss

You will need: clothes to make the boss notice you

Skimpy outfits that aren't tarty or inappropriate for the workplace, like split skirts that fall open when he walks past, are best. Don't change your attitude toward him, just flash him when the chance arises. Do this for a week only. He won't know what to do for a month after. When you've had enough, hide a stuffed animal under your skirt and when it falls open, let it fall out. Watch his expression change!

► ► ► OFFICE ◄ ◄ ◄

Become the Office Stress Manager

You will need: a clipboard and large, black-framed glasses

Offer to be the office stress manager. This will involve you walking around the office, checking that everyone is stress-free by prodding them with freshly sharpened pencils and newly manicured fingernails. Peer abruptly at your coworkers and spy on them to make sure they're working at top speed. Yell at them, "RELAX!"

● ● ● OFFICE ● ● ●

GO ON VACATION WITH NO CLOTHES

· ·

You will need: a friend with great taste who is the same size as you

· ·

It's a well-known fact that friends often have the best clothing. Find the friend closest to your size who has the best wardrobe, then ask her to come on vacation with you. "Accidentally" forget your suitcase, except for a few items of underwear and personal hygiene that you can keep in your handbag. You get both a holiday and a new cruise wardrobe without the cost or trouble.

☼ ☼ ☼ LEISURE ☼ ☼ ☼

PRACTICE EXERCISE DEFERRAL

....

You will need: a diary

....

Experts say that scheduling your workouts makes it more likely that you'll keep to a good exercise routine. Write down all the classes and times you could do at your gym. When the time comes around to take a particular class or workout time, look to the next slot of exercise you have penciled in and say, "Well, I can do that class tomorrow instead, can't I?"

☼ ☼ ☼ LEISURE ☼ ☼ ☼

Get Free Home Help

························

You will need: someone at your door

························

If someone comes to your door either wanting to sell you something or, perhaps, who has the wrong house, invite them in. Chat nicely and then feign a back ailment. Ask them politely if they would mind doing a few favors for you, seeing as you have a lumbar ailment. Before you know it, the lawn will be raked and the floors will be washed. They may even know how to bake a great apple pie.

🎇 🎇 🎇 MISCHIEF 🎇 🎇 🎇

Get Old Shoes for New

....

You will need: someone else's pair of
new shoes

....

As a nice surprise, sneak into a friend's closet and pull out
her latest pair of new shoes. No matter what size they are,
but especially if they are smaller than your size, get them
wet and force your feet into them. (If you really have
trouble, rub some oil into the leather.) Wear them for a few
days, then sneak back into her house and return them.
She'll think that she's been sleepwalking; you'll
have had new shoes for no cost.

Get Your Boyfriend to Change His Locks

························

You will need: to take a trip

························

Borrow your boyfriend's keys for some good reason and go out. Come back with them all bent up. Claim you met a conjurer who, to prove his expertise, bent your keys with mind power alone. (He also bent your pretzel, but you ate that.) When he changes the locks, get your own set, plus an extra set for when you dramatically throw yours down a drain in a fit of (pretend) jealousy or rage.

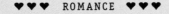

♥ ♥ ♥   ROMANCE   ♥ ♥ ♥

Get Back at Your Ex-Boyfriend

....

You will need: tiny plastic hood ornaments in
the shape of a you-know-what

....

Find out where he parks his car overnight. Fit said car
hood with tiny plastic hood ornaments that are quite
obviously a small version of the male anatomy.
It's an image that fits in so many ways.

♥♥♥ ROMANCE ♥♥♥

Win an Argument

You will need: a good memory and an ability to yell repetitively

Start an argument with someone by copying everything that they say. Yell their words back to them over and over. This will not only baffle them, it will also show them how silly their thinking is. After they flounce off, jump up and punch the air. No one will know if you won or not, but it will look as if you did.

Show Them You're a Winner

You will need: a printed sheet of paper

Start an argument that you know you'll win. On winning said argument, produce your specially printed certificate entitled "I Am a Big Loser" and get your conquered opponent to sign it. Pull a frame from your handbag and immediately put it on your desk.

Be Irish

....

You will need: a picture of two leprechauns

....

Talk in an odd accent by changing the "th" sound in words like "things" to "t." Say, "Gosh and begorra" far too often and at inappropriate moments. Show everyone pictures of your parents (use the leprechaun picture). Say that anyone who buys you a drink gets granted a special wish. When you get up to go to the restroom, say you are visiting "the pot of gold."

☙ ☙ ☙ **MISCHIEF** ☙ ☙ ☙

Turn Gifts into Cold Hard Cash

. . . .

You will need: a shop that does favors

. . . .

Many stores will exchange a gift for cash; this extends to baby shower and wedding lists, too. So find your favorite store and get into the habit of returning unwanted gifts (even if they're not yours). Not only does this spare you having to make embarrassing requests for money from people you love, it also stops your home from becoming cluttered.

🜲 🜲 🜲 MISCHIEF 🜲 🜲 🜲

Make Your Mother Love You

....

You will need: to swallow all your pride

....

Get married. Move back home. Have a child. Get a better job. Give up your job. Be a wife. Lose weight. Gain weight. Dress formally. Have your hair done the way she likes it. Agree with her. Cook. Clean. Fix the car. Before you know it, your mother will love you. But do you really, really want it that much?

☺ ☺ ☹ FAMILY ☺ ☺ ☹

Weasel in with Relatives

. . . .

You will need: lots of money and, perhaps, some moonshine

. . . .

To win over your relatives, ply them with cash as if they were bellhops and car valets. "Spoil" people with cash-enhanced attention: "Here, Auntie May," you say, flourishing a hundred-dollar bill. "Go buy yourself something nice!" Whip out a bottle of exotic booze and you'll be written into their wills overnight.

☺ ☺ ☹ FAMILY ☺ ☺ ☹

Get Help with Luggage

....

You will need: some large heavy bags and tough clothing

....

Skycaps cost too much, but who wants to handle their own luggage? Not you. While standing at the luggage carousel, look obviously nervous as you wait for your bags. When they finally show up, haphazardly try to grab the handle of the bag. Miss and fall inexpertly onto the carousel, swarming all over the bags. Someone will help you up and take your bags for you—all for free!

☼ ☼ ☼ LEISURE ☼ ☼ ☼

Go Out Wearing a Full Skirt

. . . .

You will need: a large, fully cut skirt

. . . .

So what if full skirts are (or are not) in fashion?
They're a classic and you should wear them all the
time for more reasons than that. You can hide small
children and hams underneath a large skirt; you can
ride small ponies without anyone seeing their little
feet. These skirts are also useful for stealing things,
such as small ponies.

☼ ☼ ☼ LEISURE ☼ ☼ ☼

Stop Saying the Three Scary Words

·······················

You will need: smelling salts

·······················

Do you feel like he's not saying those three little words that you'd like to hear so much? Then stop showing any signs of affection for him. Resist when he wants to kiss or more, take a sniff of the smelling salts and resist saying anything as your eyes stream. Leave the room after five minutes and when you return pretend nothing happened.

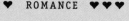

♥♥♥　ROMANCE　♥♥♥

Train Him for Success in Gift-Giving

. . . .

You will need: to be able to yell

. . . .

Take your man by the hand and show him some mannequins in a shop window. Point out that they are made of hardened material—probably plastic of some kind. Take his hand and put it on your hip. Ask him if he understands the difference between hard plastic and warm flesh. When he says he does, scream at him, "Then why did you buy me those tiny thongs that cut into my skin and make me look and feel like a human basketball?"

 ♥♥♥ ROMANCE ♥♥♥

Incentivize the Workers

You will need: a very noisy office door, a squeaky chair, and a ticking clock

Invite employees at lower employment levels than you into your office one by one. Slam your very noisy office door behind them; make them sit in the squeaky, unnerving chair; and then sit in total silence while they hear nothing but the ticking of their life draining away. They'll work so much harder after ten or fifteen minutes of sitting with you in a room devoid of normal chitchat.

← ← ← OFFICE → → →

Be Too Clean

You will need: rubber gloves, tea kettle, bucket, and sponge

Be the office tidy-bug by suddenly appearing around your rivals' desks with cleaning spray, sopping wet sponges, and large feather dusters. If they object to the mess—you will ruin a few paper objects, naturally—say, "Germs are the number one cause of company illness!" Leave everything on their desk in disarray. Better yet, move items from one desk to another.

●●● OFFICE ●●●

Day 87

Let Suede Be Your Teacher

....

You will need: a tiny spot on
any suede garment

....

Find your mother's or roommate's suede coat. Identify the

spot that's bound to be on it. Take a cloth and rub the

stain until it comes out. If that doesn't work, try licking

the spot off with your tongue. Finally, throw the garment

out, knowing that you've done all you could do. This is

important because sometimes suede is more than just a

fabric: it is a life lesson in learning how to give up.

🍒 🍒 🍒 MISCHIEF 🍒 🍒 🍒

Help Exam Jitters

....

You will need: a visit to a driving examination center

....

Walk around the waiting room, steadying nerves by making subtle statements that will keep anxiety in perspective. "I am sure that if you fail they'll let your retake it," and "A friend of mine took this test, didn't pass, and killed herself." There's always, "Oh, I've heard they made the test harder this year. The pass rate is abysmal." They'll feel they've faced the worst after seeing you.

🧨 🧨 🧨 MISCHIEF 🧨 🧨 🧨

THROW A MONKEY INTO THE FAMILY TREE

You will need: a photo or two of your siblings' kids

With your sibling, gaze at photos of their children. Say quietly, "Your kid looks so...different..." implying something awful. Continue, "No, you don't understand. They look different to other humans!" This will save you on birthday and Christmas gifts for them. Just don't expect a kidney transplant if you ever need one.

☺ ☺ ☹ FAMILY ☺ ☺ ☹

WORK THE ORPHAN SWITCH

You will need: fake adoption documents

Arrange to meet your
sister or brother. Show them pre-
aged and fake adoption documents that relate
to their birthdates. Show them the certificates,
then pull them away saying, "No, no, this is too
much!" Then yell out, "Okay, you've dragged it out
of me—you're a Romanian orphan!"

☺ ☺ ☹ FAMILY ☺ ☺ ☹

Evade That Ticket

....

You will need: a freshly written-out parking
ticket from another car

....

It's an old trick, but it works: if you are worried about
getting a parking ticket, sticking a ticket from another
car onto yours can keep the traffic cop away from your
car for up to an hour. Putting the ticket so they can't
read it easily also assists the situation.

🍒 🍒 🍒 MISCHIEF 🍒 🍒 🍒

Scare a Stranger

....

You will need: a pay phone

....

Choose a phone number at random and call. When someone answers ask in a childish voice, "Are you my mommy? Mommy? Is that you? Are you my mommy? Where are you, Mommy?" Then laugh spookily and hang up. Repeat until bored.

❧ ❧ ❧ **MISCHIEF** ❧ ❧ ❧

Look After Your Ex's Social Diary

....

You will need: his voice-mail code and
e-mail account password

....

Sure, you have no feelings for this man anymore, but that
doesn't mean you can't help out his social life a little by
deleting messages from other women on his voice-mail and
permanently deleting potentially romantic e-mails. It
should only take a few hours of sorting through his
personal life to make him a better man.

♥♥♥ ROMANCE ♥♥♥

Be the Best Lover Ever

· ·

You will need: a small notepad or a really
good memory

· ·

Men like flattery. Big surprise, huh? You, too, can make a
man think he's the best by being the "best" he's ever been
with, i.e., fake it a lot. Make everything he does "just the
best," even if that means oohing and ahhing at gnarly
cuticles, slobbering, and bad breath. Look, you're
the one who wants him, not me.

♥ ♥ ♥   ROMANCE   ♥ ♥ ♥

Steal a Taxi

. . . .

You will need: to be in a hurry

. . . .

Stand next to someone looking for a taxi. When one stops, jump in front and offer it to the person standing next to you. After they thank you and are about to get in, say, "Wait a minute! What am I doing? I need to get there faster than YOU." Throw them out of the cab and tell the driver to step on it.

❀ ❀ ❀ ETIQUETTE ❀ ❀ ❀

Support a Friend Through a Breakup

....

You will need: a list of things you didn't like
about the ex

....

Tell a pal her boyfriend's been cheating on her. "He never
wants children, especially with you! He told me!" also
works. If you think that they might get back together
though, commiserate softly. "He really hated soup," you
can say, safe in the knowledge that you haven't said
anything too radical.

❀ ❀ ❀ ETIQUETTE ❀ ❀ ❀

USE HER ROMANTIC PAST AGAINST HER

. . . .

You will need: the identity and location of your sister's big high-school crush

. . . .

Find out who your sister had a crush on in high school, find him, and seduce him. Next time she's criticizing your work or making your parents turn against you, mention this fling. That should shut her up. You can always do it with your sister's husband as well.

☺ ☻ ☹ FAMILY ☺ ☻ ☹

BLAME THE GENE POOL

························

You will need: a schematic drawing of errant
behavior in your family

························

Call your parents and bitch about your siblings, but don't
rail against the people you had to grow up with. Instead,
make it sound as if you take their side. Use passive-
aggressive criticism. "I know Billy can't help being a
shopaholic," you say. "After all, he is so sensitive and
creative. Maybe people like Billy use family money to
sustain their habits. But I would never blame Dad or you
for being bad parents. Other people may say that,
but I wouldn't."

☺ ☺ ☹ FAMILY ☺ ☺ ☹

Be Pregnant and Righteous

....

You will need: to be pregnant (or look
as if you are)

Inevitably someone will poke your tummy—people will
do it out of pure jealousy. Grab their breasts and make
as if you are turning on the taps. Explain nothing. Just
look them straight in the eye and say, "Oh, I guess it is
International Personal Space Invaders' Day, is it?"

🐞 🐞 🐞 MISCHIEF 🐞 🐞 🐞

Make Money Out of a Public Argument

....

You will need: a cup or hat with a few coins in it

....

Don't be embarrassed to have an argument in public—use it to your advantage. Encourage an argument with a friend or boyfriend. After they've gone, turn to the crowd who observed the fight and thank them for their attention. Pass around the hat/cup at the end of your thank-you and ask for money to fund your next bit of live performance art.

💣 💣 💣 **MISCHIEF** 💣 💣 💣

Arrange Your Romantic Backup

....

You will need: your own mode of transportation and a tight lip

....

Spend the day sorting out the right man for the right job. After all, few men can be everything we need. Enter their names and numbers in a black book to make sure you ask the right man for the right job—one for sex, another for socializing, yet another for shopping, still another for listening, that elusive one for potential marriage, etc. Use them for their strengths, but always find your own ride home—unless you know a chauffeur.

♥♥♥ ROMANCE ♥♥♥

Pack the Perfect Picnic

....

You will need: a bag of ants

....

Arrange a romantic picnic. Pack knives, spoons, roasted
chicken, napkins, water, wine, fresh bread, and—oh yes—
don't forget the ants. A bag of ants will make
any man at a picnic, especially an urban picnic held
on concrete, a superhero. He'll spend all the time
whacking ants while you sip the Chablis.

♥ ♥ ♥   ROMANCE   ♥ ♥ ♥

Deal with the Office Nag

You will need: to work on your grip strength

Every office has one: the person who prods you to get your attention, then grabs onto your arm when you try to get away. Rather than say, "Please don't grab on to me," grasp her hand with force and bend it backward, saying, "See, there's bad touching and good touching! Let go rapidly and look at her with an innocent eye. "So, you were saying?"

Give a Coworker a Surprise

You will need: a copy of her real birth certificate

Obtain a copy of the birth certificate for someone at work you dislike (or at random) from the records' office and produce said document at lunchtime. Read it with a loud voice and say, "Oh, here it is, Bessie Lou Fischer, only 45 years young. Doesn't she look good, folks?!? Good enough to pass for, shall we say, 35?!"

HELP A CHARITY WORKER

....

You will need: some cans to open

....

Carry some cans to a shelter or hostel. Find
a volunteer worker and ask them to open the
cans you brought—hiding the can opener first.
Offer them a Swiss Army knife to do all 45 cans.
Now they understand what helping out at
a charity is all about.

❀ ❀ ❀ ETIQUETTE ❀ ❀ ❀

GET WEDDING GIFTS FOR FREE

....

You will need: a sharp eye for the gift
table at the reception

....

Wedding gifts aren't cheap. That's why it is essential
that you are seen to give only the very best by
watching for the wealthiest and most tasteful couple
at the wedding and swapping the tags on your gift
for theirs. That way, you'll look good and they won't
know until they receive a baffling thank-you
note from the newlyweds.

❀ ❀ ❀ ETIQUETTE ❀ ❀ ❀

PLAY ONE-UPMANSHIP WITH MAKEUP

....

You will need: a worn-out bit of old makeup
with the label worn off

....

When with your catty friends, coolly place your "exotic"
bit of makeup on the counter as you dig in your
handbag for something else. Tell them this is the
best makeup you've ever used. Make a fuss about how
hard to get it is, how expensive it is, and that this is
how Julia Roberts looks so good. Be sure that your
friends can't read the Maybelline insignia, even if
they look really closely.

☼ ☼ ☼ LEISURE ☼ ☼ ☼

BUY THE BEST BRA

. . . .

You will need: about eight hours to shop
properly and a man to pay

A decent foundation garment can give you breasts
where there were none, and no hips where there were
some. No matter how long it takes, however, you will
always eventually end up with the most expensive,
cutest, and most uncomfortable selection in
Christendom. Still, if you burst into tears, this might at
least speed your boyfriend's wallet into action.

☼ ☼ ☼ LEISURE ☼ ☼ ☼

Babysit a Favorite Nephew

....

You will need: a child who is just learning sentences

....

Offer to babysit your little nephew despite the fact that you've had run-ins before. While the parents are away, drill the child with sentences that are all wrong and/or nonsensical. "Me Dadoo Catface Runs to the Cabbage Patch" is a good place to start. The child will, no doubt, be in special education by nightfall.

☺ ☺ ☹ FAMILY ☺ ☺ ☹

Tidy Up Dad's Stuff

· ·

You will need: gloves, fancy cookies, etc.

· ·

Somewhere, for some reason, your
dad will have a bunch of tins with pictures of
delicious foods on them, that are filled with nails and
greasy iron things. Why? Empty out those tins with nails
and refill them with cookies or delicious foods. Check
all of his tins for the correct contents and
amend as needed.

☺ ☺ ☹ FAMILY ☺ ☺ ☹

Eradicate Your Imperfections

....

You will need: a trusting friend with whom
to go on vacation

....

Hate vacation photos of yourself? Vacation with a pal who
likes taking photos and offer to have the film developed.
Have all the less-than-beautiful ones of you Photoshopped
to look perfect—slim thighs, flat stomach, perfect hair—
then give her the photos. "Ah, yes, just a little sun and
exercise does the trick for me," you say.

❀ ❀ ❀ ETIQUETTE ❀ ❀ ❀

Visit a New Mother

....

You will need: someone who's just given birth

....

Giving birth is exhausting. Go in and see the new baby
and help the mother out of her post-natal depression.
Make amusing remarks such as, "Wow, so many fat women!
Natural birth, eh? Well, sitting on a barstool is out for
you for a few years." Moan about your skinny ass—she's
bound to appreciate your attempts to make her feel
better about her fat one.

❀ ❀ ❀ ETIQUETTE ❀ ❀ ❀

Get an Apartment Condemned

....

You will need: a fake mustache, a building inspector's badge, a hard hat, a clipboard, and a big sign saying CONDEMNED

....

Go to the apartment of someone whom you never liked. Show your badge and gain entrance. While inside, make a list of bad things about the apartment that will need fixing: "bad color wallpaper" or "possible mouse infestation," for example. As you leave, inform the occupant that they must leave immediately. Slap the Condemned sign on the front door. They won't be able to get through to city hall about this for weeks.

🔥 🔥 🔥 🔥 MISCHIEF 🔥 🔥 🔥 🔥

Ruin a Movie Ending

....

You will need: to see all current movie releases

....

Go to a movie theater lobby and you will overhear someone talking about seeing a film. Immediately put an end to their miserable discussion by telling them the ending of the film they're about to watch. (For help, check out www.ruinedendings.com.)

☙ ☙ ☙ MISCHIEF ☙ ☙ ☙

Reverse the Push-Pull Door Signs

You will need: a screwdriver and a moment alone

It is amusing to swap the Push and Pull signs on the executive bathroom door or any other threshold over which top executives who don't know the office doors by heart may tread. Switching the signs sends a subtle message: this business is in trouble.

Be Safety Wise

You will need: several large white signs

Find a tiny step. Make it more obvious to those who
may not know about it by putting up a large sign
saying, "Look out for the step!" Put up another sign
saying, "Be careful of the step!" You may
want to rig up a movement-sensitive alarm
with a spoken warning that says, "Look out for
the step!" People will be so distracted by the signs
and alarms they are bound to discover
the step, one way or another.

●►► OFFICE ●►►

Be Impolite

....

You will need: someone who talks incessantly

....

Seek out the office/house windbag and ask them sincerely,
"How are you?" then proceed to talk over their response.
Say how you are, interrupt them, and basically don't listen
to a word they say. Then, give them a second to say
something, glance down at your watch, and say,
"My, look at the time. Must go. Sorry to hear
about the male pattern baldness."

🖤 🖤 🖤 MISCHIEF 🖤 🖤 🖤

Get Fit and Get Revenge at the Same Time

....

You will need: fake personal trainer certificate, two passes to a gym

....

Why not heal a rift with an old friend by posing as a newly commissioned personal trainer? Take your friend to the gym and help them do some metabolism-boosting weight training. If you've done your work properly (i.e., far too much), then they won't be able to walk or lift their arms above their head for days.

BECOME A WINE EXPERT

....

You will need: a small cup hung
around your neck on a chain

....

Show up at a good restaurant with your own

sommelier's cup on a chain. Look over the wine

menu and make murmurs such as, "Ah, a red one.

Hmmmm," or "Wonder what that's like?" and

"This one goes well with elk, I'm told." Insist on

tasting every wine in your little cup and return

the first two as being "too wet."

❈ ❈ ❈ ETIQUETTE ❈ ❈ ❈

Day 120

VISIT A FRIEND
IN THE HOSPITAL

....

You will need: some grapes or candy,
flowers, and a cell phone

....

Go to a hospital at visiting time and visit with
anyone who looks like they need company. Take
grapes and candy, and eat as they watch. Bring
flowers and spend hours arranging them
yourself. Speak loudly on your cell phone
about sex to remind them of what they
have to look forward to.

❀ ❀ ❀ ETIQUETTE ❀ ❀ ❀

Test His Ingenuity

....

You will need: some frozen dinners for your partner

....

Arrange to eat together tonight but then be late coming home. Leave him a note about what's in the freezer, describing it as "a delicious pizza pie" or "an irresistible lasagne" only put, in very large letters, extremely old freezing eat-by dates. Mark the packets "EAT BEFORE 12/3/89." See if he eats it anyway.

♥♥♥　ROMANCE　♥♥♥

Let a Man Know Someone Else Cares

....

You will need: a pair of sexy underwear

....

Wearing slinky, nice underwear for your man is one of the best and most subtle ways of letting him know you care. So leave that brand-new, lovely pair of panties and bra out on the bed. Add a little message in someone else's handwriting that says "Can't wait to see you in these." When confronted, say they're from your mother.

♥ ♥ ♥　ROMANCE　♥ ♥ ♥

Help an Adult Talk to a Child

· ·

You will need: a stupid adult and a child

Find someone talking to a child, interrupt them, and
quote "a recent study" that proves that speaking
intelligently to the child works best. Then have a lovely
conversation about the periodic table with said infant.
If the adult is speaking in adult tones to the baby,
interrupt and converse in nothing but "goo-goo, ga-ga"
to the child, citing a different "recent study."

♦ ♦ ♦ MISCHIEF ♦ ♦ ♦

Live the Dream

· ·

You will need: sunglasses, a sweeping coat, and the word "darling"

· ·

Even if you can't afford a cup of coffee, you can pretend to "be someone" by wearing sunglasses and a stylish, make-a-statement coat everywhere you go. Brandish the word "darling" every chance you get and folks will wonder, "Who is that? Should we know her? Is she famous?"

🎇 🎇 🎇 MISCHIEF 🎇 🎇 🎇

Give Your Boss the Gift That Keeps Giving

You will need: a solar-powered stereo

Everyone loves the sound of music in their office. So give your boss the gift of a solar-powered stereo that plays a tune such as "Music Box Dancer" or perhaps a song from *Mary Poppins*. Be sure to break the Off switch before you give it as a gift. It won't stop until its solar batteries run out—in about a hundred years.

◆◆◆ OFFICE ◆◆◆

Start an Anthrax Scare

You will need: to mail yourself an envelope containing face powder

When things get dull at work, liven things up by opening an envelope of white powder so strenuously that it flies everywhere—over you and anyone sitting near you. Scream and run to the toilet with the bag—it has to be destroyed so there's no evidence linking the closure of your workplace for several days to you. Tell anyone who asks that you panicked.

●●● OFFICE ●●●

Create a Special Name

....

You will need: a name that is easy to mangle

....

Rename yourself something difficult ("Alisha" or
"Scavflug" or some such). Make it clear that anyone who
mispronounces your name is the worst criminal
imaginable. In fact, say that "Mispronouncing my
name is the worst crime imaginable." Get very upset
when anyone gets your name wrong.

❋❋❋ ETIQUETTE ❋❋❋

Comfort the Bride

....

You will need: to get the bride alone

....

Find a wedding in process. Pull the bride aside and, in conspiratorial tones, inform her that there was a large bug crawling up her dress and it ruined the whole ceremony because no one could take their eyes off it. Tell her, too, that her dress looked like something out of the movie *Grease*, although you really like that two-tone look. Give her tissues when she starts to cry.

❀ ❀ ❀ ETIQUETTE ❀ ❀ ❀

Take the Maypole Position

....

You will need: an actual Maypole, but perhaps substitute any old pole if pushed

....

Early this morning, thread and weave large ribbons around a telephone pole in your street. Wearing a plain white, see-through smock or nightgown, yell loudly until everyone comes out of their houses. Encourage neighbors to dance around your Maypole singing lusty songs. The men will probably be more willing than the women. Sneak away and call the cops.

☙ ☙ ☙ **MISCHIEF** ☙ ☙ ☙

Surprise a Vegetarian

. . . .

You will need: beef minced into tiny itsy bitsy pieces and ingredients for a chocolate cake

. . . .

Find a vegetarian who'll eat chocolate cake and invite them over for coffee and cake. Make it really special for them and put some small bits of beef into the cake. They needn't notice and they'll certainly be subconsciously grateful for the extra protein and iron they'll be getting.

🧨 🧨 🧨 **MISCHIEF** 🧨 🧨 🧨

DON'T GROW UP

. . . .

You will need: a schoolgirl's uniform and hair in braids

. . . .

Arrange an impromptu family get-together at your place.
Bake cookies badly and have warm milk. Talk with a slight
lisp and throw a tantrum as soon as anyone asks what's
wrong with you. Accuse siblings of hitting, kicking, or
biting you and wail for Mom. Now they'll listen
when you say you want your own life.

☺ ☹ ☺ FAMILY ☺ ☹ ☺

Day 132

QUIT SMOKING

....

You will need: to smoke (start, if necessary)

....

Dad knows how bad smoking is for you, so he'll help you to stop. Ask him to pay for scuba diving, diving, flying, and skydiving classes—they're all difficult to combine with smoking. If he really loved you, tell him, he'd pay for all of them.

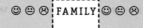 FAMILY ☺ 😐 ☹

Charity Vengeance

....

You will need: a charity vest and a clipboard

....

Stand outside your ex's place of work and try to get people to give you money for whatever charity you're working for. Volunteer for long shifts: eventually, you know he has to come out of the building, wherein you pounce on him, saying, "Look! Look what you've done to me! You left and I'm here begging—and I don't even get to keep the money. How sad is that?"

♥♥♥   ROMANCE   ♥♥♥

Sidestep the Prenuptial

....

You will need: a prenup agreement and
a really good doctor

....

Call your partner and suggest getting a prenuptial
agreement signed today. Meanwhile, get a doctor friend (or
a good forger) to certify you as clinically unfit mentally
for legal or moral decision making, and you're in the clear
for getting everything from your partner—even if your
name is on that dotted line.

♥♥♥ ROMANCE ♥♥♥

REDESIGN YOUR BODY

. . . .

You will need: a large variety of
undergarments and marshmallows

. . . .

Hate your small breasts but afraid of surgery? Try
stuffing your bra with large, squishy white
marshmallows. Want hips but can't gain weight? Try
stuffing marshmallows into a large pair of panties. Want
a bigger bottom? Put marshmallows into your pants and
sit down repeatedly to shape them to your form. Don't
use tissues and cloth padding; opt for edible items in
case you get caught. "These? Oh, I LOVE sweets!"

☼ ☼ ☼ LEISURE ☼ ☼ ☼

SHOP IN THE SALES: 2

....

You will need: a fake tattoo, a toothpick,
some tooth-blackener

....

Although few things stop a veteran shopper, looking
tougher than the average woman can give you an edge.
Chew on a toothpick as you riffle through the scarves;
show off your tattoo (DAD) while pawing through the
swimsuits. Show that you have several teeth missing
and don't care. Mutter, "This is worse than the big
house," under your breath. Everyone will give you
plenty of shopping space.

☼ ☼ ☼ LEISURE ☼ ☼ ☼

AVOID TALKING TO ANYONE

You will need: a set of
portable earphones

Before leaving home this morning, put on a set
of old earphones and you'll be blissfully free of
any liability to speak to anyone. It doesn't
matter that you have nothing plugged into the
end of the phones—nobody need know.

❋ ❋ ❋ ETIQUETTE ❋ ❋ ❋

GIVE THE PERFECT WEDDING GIFT

....

You will need: a card with the top of
the envelope slit open

....

There are lots of weddings announced in your local
newspaper. Find one and take a sealed card to it,
but before you get there, slit the top of the
envelope open. Tell anyone who'll listen that, "I put
a couple of hundred-dollar bills in my card." This
makes you look very generous and their people look
very shifty indeed.

❀ ❀ ❀   ETIQUETTE   ❀ ❀ ❀

Day 139

Be a Patriot

....

You will need: time to shop for nationally produced goods only

....

Today buy things made only in America. This means you should not purchase any electrical products or anything fashionable (as all of those will either be from China or Europe). Today is a good day to persuade everyone you know to buy—er, uh, wait a minute, maybe, no, ah yes—soap! Made right here in your country.

🧨 🧨 🧨 MISCHIEF 🧨 🧨 🧨

Boycott a Vegetarian Restaurant

....

You will need: the courage of your convictions and a sign saying, "Free the Spinach"

....

Killing is wrong. We all know this. And yet, even so-called vegetarians kill defenseless vegetables and soy beans every day of their lives. Don't let them get away with this senseless slaughter of the innocents. Walk up and down the pavement outside a vegetarian restaurant, crying, "Carrot killer!"

🌑 🌑 🌑 MISCHIEF 🌑 🌑 🌑

TAKE UP RUNNING

You will need: someone to pay for all that expensive gear

Running is very good
for you. Tell your parents that a
doctor pal said that you should start because of
your family genes. Get them to buy you some
running shoes, shorts, a tank top, and so on. In a
few weeks you can claim that you're marathon
training and need to go to South America to
"train." They'll be so happy you're doing
something that they'll pay for the flight.

☺ ☺ ☹ FAMILY ☺ ☺ ☹

TEACH YOUR PARENTS ABOUT FONDUE

You will need: a fondue pot and some boiling water

Invite Mom and Pop to dinner. Throw boiling water into the fondue pot. Do not light the fondue pot. Take bits of raw meat and marshmallows, skewer them onto the forks, then dip into the hot water. Put them out after a few minutes and say, "Isn't this what you used to make? It isn't very nice. No wonder fondue pots are always at garage sales."

☺ ☺ ☹ FAMILY ☺ ☺ ☹

Be a Complete Diva

· ·

You will need: people who give two hoots about you

To be a real diva, you need to complain about everything, but the best divas complain about something measurable: temperature is your best choice. Complain about the temperature of your dress. Bitch about the temperature of your drink. Moan about the cold air on your face caused by your false eyelashes.

🖤 🖤 🖤 MISCHIEF 🖤 🖤 🖤

Be Historically Correct

....

You will need: a window and a pile of animal dung (preferably horse)

....

The Defenestration of Prague is an actual historical event when a few Czech royals were thrown out of a window and survived by landing in a pile of excrement. Reenact this historical event by piling some manure outside your window and pushing your best friend through the window into the manure below.

💣💣💣 MISCHIEF 💣💣💣

Help Everyone Eat Healthier

You will need: a calorie counter

Trying to eat right isn't easy, but with a little knowledge everyone can eat healthier. Learn the calorie count of common foods and tell everyone that you see eating how many calories they're taking in. After a few days your coworkers will be healthier, thinner, and a lot more angry—which is more good news since they'll burn more calories.

Read the Stars

You will need: a horoscope column from any newspaper or magazine

Everyone knows that astrology is hooey. But just in case it isn't, read out daily horoscopes to everyone in the office—with some extras you put in personally. "Pisces: a great day with Saturn in your mid-heaven, but look out because the boss knows you're stealing money from petty cash." That'll keep them on their toes.

● ● ● OFFICE ● ● ●

Change a Religion

· ·

You will need: a truly confused expression

Go into any place of worship and throw yourself into their rituals—then ask for a few changes. Communion? Sure, if they have Atkins carb-free wafers. Donation? You already gave: you put the money in the wishing well/holy water font. Wear something on your head? Why? And ruin this hairdo? Do not worship craven images? Does advertising count?

◆ ◆ ◆ MISCHIEF ◆ ◆ ◆

Remember Someone

....

You will need: a photo album full of pictures of you with ex-boyfriends

....

Create your own version of Memorial Day by getting out your photo albums and trying to remember who everyone is. Look through it with your boyfriend. He'll love seeing all your old boyfriends from college. Then try to remember the names of everyone you've ever slept with and write a list.

💣 💣 💣 MISCHIEF 💣 💣 💣

Handle the, Er, Not-That-Ugly Baby

....

You will need: to be confronted with a truly hideous baby

....

Go to a maternity ward or playground. When confronted with a baby that, by rights, should be left at home, try to say something positive and uplifting. Say something like, "Gee, he sure has his father's genes!" or "You know, you shouldn't really blame yourself." Parents know deep down inside their child is ugly. Really.

❀ ❀ ❀ ETIQUETTE ❀ ❀ ❀

Get Ahead in the Restaurant Line

....

You will need: to be behind someone in a restaurant line

....

In a restaurant reachable only by automotive means, get a table faster by telling the person ahead of you, "Hey! They're towing your car!" They'll leave the line and you'll get their table. Perfect. N.B. If they come in mad, say, "But I was sure I saw you getting out of that car! Man, I'm just trying to help here, okay? Sheesh."

❀ ❀ ❀ **ETIQUETTE** ❀ ❀ ❀

Ruin a Wedding

....

You will need: a bridal gown

....

There's nothing quite like showing up at a wedding just as the bride is about to say "I do" and running down the aisle, holding your dress and screaming, "Wait! Wait! You've got the wrong girl!" There's nothing illegal about it. Anyway, if you dislike her or him or just need to have a little fun, this is the best way to make that day memorable for everyone involved.

💣 💣 💣 **MISCHIEF** 💣 💣 💣

Be a Tour Guide

· ·

You will need: a bullhorn

· ·

Find out where the celebrities stay in your town, where the most famous murder happened, or where there is sometimes a puddle of water where one shouldn't be. Better yet, get a guide to another city and memorize that. Using the bullhorn, walk the streets broadcasting the wrong bits of historical information from the wrong architectural period and, indeed, the wrong city.

❧ ❧ ❧ ❧ **MISCHIEF** ❧ ❧ ❧ ❧

Day 153

Get Him to Wear Your Panties

....

You will need: big Bridget Jones-style
panties

....

If a man likes you in big ugly underwear, or so the story
goes, he will like you in anything. In fact, he probably
loves you. So get him to prove it by wearing your big
panties all day, to work. Then phone his pal and tell
him what your guy's doing.

❤❤❤ ROMANCE ❤❤❤

Label His Shorts

....

You will need: a marker and clothing labels

....

Sew a label on the back of each and every one of his
underpants' waistbands. Mark his pants with his name
and your address. His underwear is now marked so
he remembers who he is and where he belongs after
a long night out. It is also there in case any woman
may run across him with only his skivvies on. She
needs to see your brand. And there it is.

♥ ♥ ♥   ROMANCE   ♥ ♥ ♥

Bridge the Men-and-Lingerie Chasm of Taste

. . . .

You will need: a whip and some cookies

. . . .

Most men couldn't buy the right lingerie if their lives depended on it. Bring a little of that power to bear by training your man to choose good underwear by using a whip and a tray of cookies. Show him a lingerie catalog and ask him to pick out his favorite ones. If he gets it right, give him a cookie. If he gets it wrong, snap a whip at him. He'll soon get the hang of it.

✿ ✿ ✿ **LEISURE** ✿ ✿ ✿

Date Like You Don't Need Lovin'

....

You will need: a gullible boyfriend

....

Why wait until you're without a boyfriend to find another? Wise women line up potentials like some South American millionaires line up polo ponies. Start scoping parties, launches, meetings, and holidays for future sex snacks. You'll be glad you did.

✿ ✿ ✿ LEISURE ✿ ✿ ✿

Play a Practical Joke

....

**You will need: a squeezy tube of toothpaste
with a removable cap**

....

Put just a bit of liquid kitchen sink cleanser into the
toothpaste. Sure, it's poison, but a bit won't kill them.
The cleanser is bound to give them a brighter smile—
and everyone should be able to laugh at a prank like
that. Even if they're sitting in the Emergency Room.

🍒 🍒 🍒 MISCHIEF 🍒 🍒 🍒

Meet New People

....

You will need: contempt for beliefs not
your own

....

Find your local Jehovah's Witness center. It might be
called a church. Offer them your services as a spreader
of the word. Take many copies of *The Watchtower* and go
visiting. Total strangers will either abuse you or ask you
into their home. The abusers you can abuse back. Once
inside anyone's home, abuse them for being too trusting
in this day and age.

💣 💣 💣 **MISCHIEF** 💣 💣 💣

Confirm Your Suspicious

....

You will need: a pair of lady's underwear

....

If you suspect that your boyfriend is cheating on you, stuff a pair of foreign underwear into his pocket, in his car's glove compartment, or into his soup. When he discovers them—hopefully when you are there—watch his face. When you ask, "Whose are those?" look to see if he's lying or not. If his lips move, he's guilty.

♥♥♥ ROMANCE ♥♥♥

Choose Your Lucky Charm Underpants

. . . .

You will need: a cute pair of panties

. . . .

Everyone has a lucky charm, even if they don't know it. Make your own by wearing the same pair of cute underpants to every great event in your life. Choose the pair to wear to your wedding, the birth of your child, your divorce, and your triumph in divorce court. Let your partner know you've made the choice and show him.

♥ ♥ ♥ ROMANCE ♥ ♥ ♥

Be a Concerned Citizen

You will need: a daily newspaper

Accuse your boss of not being reasonable or a man of the world. Pointing to a newspaper, say, "You only read the paper for the sports and the finance section. Oh, and maybe the cars. You're not like me. I'm involved in the world. I am concerned about global education, learning, and knowledge. I want us to emerge from the dark ages into the light of reason."

Draw an Unflattering Caricature of Your Boss

You will need: a pencil and eraser

It's going to be a lovely day—why would you want to spend it in the office? Remember how you used to get sent from the classroom when the sketch of your teacher with wonky eyes and a fat ass was spied by her? Well, you can get the same result by making the same sketch of your boss! Pin it on the notice board after signing it.

Enjoy the day!

◄◄◄ OFFICE ►►►

Prevent the Wedding

....

You will need: to pretend to be in love with your best friend's man

....

Tell her that you love him, but she got him first. Then ask to be a bridesmaid. Tell her that when they ask if anyone objects to the union, you won't pay someone in the audience to yell, "He's in love with someone else! And so is she!" Shocked and worried, your pal may never become the bride now! And she'll never attempt to steal a man from you again.

🎇 🎇 🎇 MISCHIEF 🎇 🎇 🎇

Feed a Vegan

....

You will need: whatever is the vegetable equivalent of gravel

....

Invite a vegan "friend" to dinner. Don't bother going to the health food store to get kasha, Kamut, quinoa, or barley. Health food stores are far too refined for this: go directly to the feed store and purchase some top-quality pet kibble and horse feed. Boil lightly and serve. Add salt if your guest is picky. They'll have the cleanest colon in the world.

🖤 🖤 🖤 MISCHIEF 🖤 🖤 🖤

Fake It Badly

....

You will need: a sarcastic tone of voice

....

Start moaning loudly but in a flat tone as soon as he starts making love to you. Tell him in a very sarcastic voice that he's the one, your big boy. Tell him, "Oh do it to me harder." Then yawn, pretending to stifle it. If he gets upset, tell him that sarcasm really turns you on. But only your sarcasm, not his.

 **♥♥♥ ROMANCE ♥♥♥**

Have a Successful Affair

....

You will need: to have an affair

....

When you have an affair, take responsibility for all your
orgasms, great times, thrills, and chills. When you follow
any of the advice in this book, and you find yourself
asking, "Was it worth doing?" Just think, "How long am
I going to be dead?" Comfort yourself with the fact that
the damage you will cause by following the advice in this
book could last for generations.

♥♥♥ ROMANCE ♥♥♥

MAKE A WEDDING SPECIAL

....

You will need: a great line of flattery

....

Weddings are stressful times. Employ more flattery than usual to make yourself known to the family, the caterer, and anyone else who may give you food, money, or love. Slap the father on the back and offer to buy him a drink. He'll be grateful for the offer but, by custom, unable to take you up on it. Instead he'll buy you a magnum of champagne.

❀ ❀ ❀ ETIQUETTE ❀ ❀ ❀

IMPROVE YOUR EX-BOYFRIEND'S REPUTATION

....

You will need: a photographic memory

....

Find out where your ex is eating tonight, then
march to the table and beg for an opportunity to
say a few words about him. His pals will love it.
Stand there and read "diary" excerpts aloud,
especially the ones about stealing from the
family, hating various pals (all present), and
cheating on his new girl with you.

❀ ❀ ❀ ETIQUETTE ❀ ❀ ❀

Be a Secret Agent

. . . .

You will need: a tedious party

We've all been to parties where there's one or two people bragging about their accomplishments. Sometimes these people are interesting and benign. Often, however, they are merely dull. So, interrupt someone else's story and start a story about yourself in an exotic location. Suddenly clamp a hand over your mouth. When asked for details, look into your drink and say, "I really can't talk about it," and walk away.

💣 💣 💣 **MISCHIEF** 💣 💣 💣

Get More Liquor for Less

....

You will need: a very large, cumbersome handbag

....

In most bars and restaurants, if you spill your drink they will often replace it without charge. To capitalize on this, you must learn to swing your large, cumbersome handbag at just the right pitch to catch that glass of wine (or better, the ice bucket with a half bottle of champagne in it), and fling it to the floor. This can be done at least once, ensuring a good time for all at half the price.

🎇 🎇 🎇 MISCHIEF 🎇 🎇 🎇

The Grocery Breakup Ploy

....

You will need: a list of ridiculous
edible items

....

Get rid of a man the easy way by sending him to the

grocery store with a list of items that he can't possibly

find. When he comes back with the wrong items—or

none—pick a fight saying that as he can't even shop right,

how are you supposed to hold the relationship together?!

♥♥♥ ROMANCE ♥♥♥

Become Bisexual

· ·

You will need: a sexy female friend

· ·

Ask your best female friend—straight or not—to act as
your extremely obvious girlfriend on a night out. When
visiting bars and clubs, act straight until guys are showing
too much interest. Then become very, very friendly with
your girlfriend. You could also offer to sell DVDs of your
"girl-on-girl action." Take cash in advance, take an
address, and then beat it.

♥♥♥ ROMANCE ♥♥♥

Give Someone Praise

You will need: someone who does their job adequately

Praise is the way to motivate workers. But how do you motivate someone who is barely adequate at their job? By praising them fulsomely and consistently, then adding, "You are doing a brilliant job, outside of losing the company a hell of a lot of money. But really, the whole office looks up to you, maybe not for that terrible mistake you made, but for many other, er, reasons..."

➤ ➤ ➤ OFFICE ➤ ➤ ➤

Be the Victim of Sexual Harassment

You will need: a horrid photocopy of someone's bottom

Late at night when no one is around, including the janitor, leave the Xerox sitting on your desk. On arrival at work the next morning, appear to be shocked and saddened that someone played such a childish and nasty prank. You'll get free coffees and sympathy from all the women for weeks after. If you play your cards right, this kindness and attention will last all year long.

● ● ● OFFICE ● ● ●

Add Spice to a Wedding

....

You will need: a shotgun

....

Find a wedding party as it's leaving the church. Join it,
holding the shotgun down by your side. When the bride
throws her bouquet, aim and then blow it out of the sky.
This will not only make the wedding memorable but also
prove your hunting prowess with all single people there.
N.B. Make sure the bouquet is thrown high enough: try not
to clip any of the bridesmaids.

❀❀❀ ETIQUETTE ❀❀❀

Drink Free Beer All Night

....

You will need: a man's suit, a pair of wing-tip shoes, and a fake mustache

....

Walk into a smart bar dressed in your man's outfit. Walk up to the bartender and announce that from now on he is to call you Butch and serve you beer with foam. When he laughs, throw the peanuts in his face and demand to see the manager. If the manager laughs, threaten to sue. Drink free beer all night.

❀ ❀ ❀ ETIQUETTE ❀ ❀ ❀

LIVE IN A FILM

....

You will need: someone to watch over you

....

Contract amnesia to the point where you only remember the phone number of a carpet company somewhere in the Chicago area. Sleep in full makeup and awake looking perfect; find an ideal parking space. These things should happen in real life but don't unless you make it so. N.B. Sometimes dream sequences are real: pinch yourself to make sure you aren't falling to your death or drowning in a flashback.

☼ ☼ ☼ LEISURE ☼ ☼ ☼

DISCOURAGE VISITORS

....

You will need: a one-person cat

....

Get a feral cat. Train it to love only you. When someone comes over, answer the door holding the cat. Invite them in and, just as you shut the door, say, "Here!" and hand them the cat. The cat will crawl and bite in an effort to get away. Shredded skin and clothes should result.

☼ ☼ ☼ LEISURE ☼ ☼ ☼

Feed a Carnivore

....

You will need: a cow or pig's head and a maraschino cherry

....

Invite your meat-eating friends over for a feast they won't forget. Go to your local butcher shop and buy a whole cow or pig's head. Cook it up in the oven and decorate with cherries. There's nothing quite like a recognizable bit of an animal to make meat-lovers all over the world sit up and take notice.

💣 💣 💣 MISCHIEF 💣 💣 💣

Storm the Vinyl Frontier

....

You will need: someone you hate who has a valuable record collection

....

Go over to the vinyl-collector's place and ask to hear a record, perhaps one of their favorites. As they play it, go a bit crazy. Get near the player—too close—and start dancing wildly. Swing your arms about, do bad imitations of old dances like the Swim, the Pony, and the Boogaloo. Jump around close enough and high enough to cause the record to skip and, if you're lucky, scratch.

Play the Furniture Game

. . . .

You will need: rickety old furniture

. . . .

Invite some people around to your house. As they seek
to find a place to sit down, steer them away from
every seat in the house by yelling, "Not that chair!" or
"Oh gosh, don't sit there!" or "Please, not the
Hepplewhite!" Set the legs of your sofa on easily
toppled blocks so that when they do go to sit down,
the whole piece drops to the floor with a "whump."

✵ ✵ ✵ LEISURE ✵ ✵ ✵

Dress with Less

. . . .

You will need: no underwear

. . . .

Going without underpants carries a certain danger.
Don't get your shoes shined, get caught in any upward
drafts, climb any ladders or stairs and you'll be fine.
So find a guy and tease him by flashing and making it
very clear that today is laundry day at your house—
and maybe he should come over. Make sure you're out
when he calls.

✺ ✺ ✺ LEISURE ✺ ✺ ✺

Scout for Dates at a Funeral

You will need: a great black dress, a veil, hat, and just the right shoes. Oh, and gloves

Find a funeral. Arrive early and sit in the back. Look for not-too-upset, good-looking victims to stand near. If there is a wake, attend it. If you're lucky, it will be an Irish, Polish, or other drinking-ethnicity wake. You'll have a boyfriend by morning. (Make sure he has a pulse, though.)

✵ ✵ ✵ LEISURE ✵ ✵ ✵

Throw the Perfect Party

....

You will need: to get very drunk

....

The only way to throw the perfect party is for you, the hostess, not to care what happens. Don't fret about the canapés or red wine stains. Have a few drinks on an empty stomach and you'll be flying. You'll learn to dance, how to shoot tequila, and how to speak Romanian all in one night. Leave an old coat out on the bed so you can wake up with something familiar in a few days.

✳✳✳ **LEISURE** ✳✳✳

SET UP A "STING" ON YOUR PARENTS

....

You will need: a male friend with no scruples

....

First thing in the morning, call your parents. Sound rushed and slightly furtive. Don't chat. Just tell them that you'll be there tomorrow and there's something important that you need to discuss. Hang up abruptly. Get your male friend to call them asking for you at ever-decreasing intervals, always refusing to leave his name. He should make the last call at midnight, sounding very angry. Meanwhile, spend the night getting drunk so that you'll look as terrible as possible in the morning.

☺ ☺ ☹ FAMILY ☺ ☺ ☹

GET YOUR INHERITANCE TODAY

. . . .

You will need: the undying love of your parents (see opposite)

. . . .

Get your male friend to resume his calls at 6 a.m. Turn up at your family home looking dreadful. Stay in the house at all times, glancing through the curtains along the street. When you can hold out no more, break down and tell your parents that you owe a lot of money to a very scary man and you have to pay it by next Sunday or you'll go missing. Ask for as much as you think they can afford. Get Dad to call your male friend and tell him he'll pay.

☺ ☻ ☹ FAMILY ☺ ☻ ☹

Have an Anti-Man Party (and a free expensive dress)

....

You will need: a sympathetic friend and a
pocket-sized voice recorder

....

Pretend that you've just dumped your boyfriend. Run over
to your friend's house crying. Throw yourself onto her sofa
and await tissues, ice cream, and sympathy. Talk about how
good you were to him and how he never really appreciated
you. Have some wine. Start laughing. Secretly record your
friend bitching about her boyfriend; play it back to her
later when you want to borrow that expensive dress.

♥♥♥ ROMANCE ♥♥♥

Flirt That Friend Away

....

You will need: a friend's husband you
fancy like mad

....

Sometimes you have to choose between your own goals
and needs, and your friends. You can always get new
friends. Goals are few and far between. So if you're totally
sure you'd rather have that man than that friend, start
hanging on your friend's boyfriend/husband. When your
friend catches you and screams, speak quietly back
to her saying, "Why are you yelling at me? Can't you
see I'm busy?!?" Make sure she has paid you that
money she owes you, too.

♥♥♥ ROMANCE ♥♥♥

Spoil an Enemy's Hair

You will need: a day at a hotel, hair dye in blond, a chlorinated swimming pool

Tell your office enemy that it is time to bury the hatchet. Suggest that you both go to a day spa where she can get her horrid platinum locks touched up as your treat. Just as she comes out of the salon, bump into her, pushing her "accidentally" into the chlorinated pool. Her hair will turn green. Instantly.

Be Profound

You will need: tiny crib notes

When things go wrong at work, have something vaguely nauseating and slightly profound to say. Your best bets are: "My best thinking got me here," "That which doesn't kill us maims us," and "Suicide is a permanent solution to a temporary problem," all uttered with a profound face. Try not to laugh.

GET FREE BEAUTY TREATMENTS

. . . .

You will need: a touchy salon staff member

. . . .

Go to a salon about which you've heard bad things. Find the most nervous salon staff member and ask her for a massage. At the end, jump up and say, "This isn't what I want! Get me the manager!" Ask for another massage for free; explain that you weren't told exactly what to expect and that you are sorely disappointed. You may also mention that your husband is the editor of the *New York Times* (make sure you know who that is).

☼ ☼ ☼ LEISURE ☼ ☼ ☼

TRIUMPH AT THE STORE

. . . .

You will need: a catsuit, sharpened elbows,
and a fake foreign accent

. . . .

Head to the store in a catsuit with your credit card in a
secure pocket. Using elbows, feet, and fists if you must,
get into the stack/rail/bin of goodies. Swear in Croatian
or Serbian. If anyone grabs an item you want yell,
"Soroya! Mea crote zaki!" It doesn't mean anything, but
it sounds terrifying coming from a catsuit-clad maniac.
Sane people will run away from you.

☼ ☼ ☼ LEISURE ☼ ☼ ☼

GET OUT OF PHYSICAL CONTACT

....

You will need: a sweater covered in dangling decorations/fake breast job

....

Go someplace where they like to HUG! Wear your special anti-contact sweater—the one with the bits of metal dangling off of it—and make it clear that hugging you is off-limits. Say, "If this weren't a piece of artwork, you know a hug would be the perfect thing." Alternatively, feign a breast job and say you can't be hugged or lift your arms. Works every time.

❀ ❀ ❀ ETIQUETTE ❀ ❀ ❀

HELP YOUR NIECE PASS HER DRIVING TEST

....

You will need: a slightly doctored *Rules of the Road* booklet

....

She never liked you and the feeling was mutual. You offer to help her study for her driving test— the written part, silly—by asking her test questions and giving her the wrong answers. Is a right turn on red legal? No, silly. Seatbelts? They're only for the passenger. What's that red triangle mean? The other guy has to let your car go first.

❀ ❀ ❀   ETIQUETTE   ❀ ❀ ❀

BABYSIT YOUR FAVORITE NEPHEW: 2

You will need: a backyard sandbox

It's time to babysit
your favorite nephew yet again.
This time, tell him you're going to play
"survive in the wild desert." This will teach him
how to survive in quicksand just like the old-time
soldiers had to. Making sure the sandbox is
well out of earshot, bury him up to the neck. Warn
him of the local dogs, ants, and cats. Check him
in an hour or so.

☺ ☺ ☹ FAMILY ☺ ☺ ☹

IMPROVE YOURSELF

You will need: four pieces of chocolate

Go up to a niece or
nephew and offer them one piece
of candy. Then eat one yourself. As you are
looking at the child, grab the other two pieces and
gobble them up really quickly. Say afterward,
"There. That's a life lesson for you." Walk away.

☺ ☺ ☹ FAMILY ☺ ☺ ☹

Be a Baby Lover

....

You will need: earplugs

....

Get onboard a plane or a train, talking all the while with
your friend about how much you love children, how you
adore your brother's kids, and how you miss yours at home.
Tell them that you don't understand how anyone could be
mean to children; after all, they are our future and they're
so sweet and loving and innocent. But the minute any
child near you makes a noise, call over the steward and
demand a new seat away from the "loud-mouthed brat."

❀ ❀ ❀ ETIQUETTE ❀ ❀ ❀

Win the Good Person Award

....

You will need: a sort of competition between your friends as to who is the most charitable

....

Let all your friends know that you are dressing up as Santa Claus this Christmas and visiting ailing boys and girls as well as spending hours down at the local department store. Don't tell them that the only reason you're doing this is so you get a chance to drink in public: you can stash a lot of liquor in that belly.

Make an Instant Female Friend

....

You will need: a long list of bad things

....

To make a female stranger a friend, remember to talk about three topics: your relationships, your family, and your body. "My partner's bathroom habits—oy!" Or try the popular combination of mother and body in one: "My mother hates my hair! All my life she tried to curl it with hot tongs. Hot tongs?! I was three years old!" No woman can fail to be your friend after that. She may even weep a bit.

☼ ☼ ☼ **LEISURE** ☼ ☼ ☼

Ballroom Dance

. . . .

You will need: a long, annoying gown

. . . .

Go to a ballroom. Wear the longest, most irritating gown you can find. Get someone to ask you to dance and then do the best you can, blaming the dress for your inability to coast smoothly around the dance floor. No one will know that you've got two left feet, no sense of rhythm, and that the only dancing you ever did was square.

☼ ☼ ☼ LEISURE ☼ ☼ ☼

Date a Younger Man

....

You will need: a grill, a game, and a beer

....

Invite any young man over to your house and offer to cook dinner. Slap some chicken on the grill, give him the remote control, and open up a beer. Say little or nothing to him all night until he makes a move. He will think he died and went to heaven. He'll be your slave from that night onward.

♥ ♥ ♥   ROMANCE   ♥ ♥ ♥

Confuse a Nice if Dull Man

....

You will need: a man who is, er, nice but dull

....

Identify your nice but dull man. Tell him that you just
don't have time anymore for a good man like him, that it
isn't fair to keep stringing him along, and that you love
him too much to have him put up with your busy schedule.
Tell him you are also thinking about joining a convent in
Bolivia where they don't allow men who look like him.

Walk away with a sob.

♥♥♥   ROMANCE   ♥♥♥

Defeat a Sensible Argument

You will need: one perfect catchphrase

If confronted with a really good sensible argument, do not succumb to reason. When someone says to you that they are trying to be fair and moderate, look them straight in the eye and say, "I don't value those things." With one fell swoop, you have won the argument—and, probably, some contempt.

Exaggerate a Medical Problem

You will need: no conscience whatsoever

Get coworkers talking about their illnesses at lunch. About an hour in, tell them about a friend who had a similar problem. In fact, she had an identical problem. Her solution? Make it radical. Throw in some juicy details, "Then her nose turned blue! No! Really! Then she couldn't stop hiccuping." They'll spill all to try and match the made-up story you've just told.

● ● ● OFFICE ● ● ●

Empty the Beach of Volleyball Players

. . . .

You will need: a crowded beach where happy, beautiful folks are playing volleyball

. . . .

Go to where the other people are playing. Run around them yelling, "I got it!" Barge into them and cock your wrist as if you are about to spike the ball. Continue until they think you are a sociopath. Sooner or later, they will leave you alone on the beach.

🌑 🌑 🌑 MISCHIEF 🌑 🌑 🌑

Buy the Perfect Educational Child's Gift

....

You will need: an obviously cheap child's toy

....

Children these days take things for granted. So buy a child a gift that will self-destruct in minutes. This will not only teach him to appreciate gifts but also to endure the wrath of his parents—who will think he broke it on purpose because he doesn't like you—AND it will get him to recognize the futility of life.

🔥🔥🔥 **MISCHIEF** 🔥🔥🔥

Dump a Man without Telling Him It's Over

....

You will need: to lie through your teeth

....

Date a man, make it clear you want the relationship to be exclusive, then don't see him for a few weeks. Go out and kiss everyone you can lay your lips on. Make sure they put their hands all over your body. It will only take a few days for your date to hear that you've been out carousing while he's been home being faithful to you. Tell him you can't believe how clingy and needy he's being. Say, "Sheesh" a few times for effect.

 ♥♥♥ ROMANCE ♥♥♥

Get Better Treatment from Your Partner

....

You will need: to wake him up without seeming to be awake yourself

....

Go to sleep. In the middle of the night, thump your partner with your arm and say the name of your ex. "Gerald!" you cry out, "Gerald!" Sigh a long, satisfied sigh as you peep one eye open to see if he's listening. If you hear the sound of snoring, start back at the beginning. This time hit him harder and yell louder.

♥♥♥   ROMANCE   ♥♥♥

GET PAID FOR VACATIONING BY THE LAKE

. . . .

You will need: a new friend with a cabin
by the lake

. . . .

Find out when the cabin is empty. Plant skunks inside.
Tell your new friend that you have, coincidentally,
started a skunk-removal service. Say that you'll be glad
to give them a discounted service but that it could take
up to three weeks to rid the cabin of those smelly
varmints. You'll get paid for having a great summer.

☼ ☼ ☼ LEISURE ☼ ☼ ☼

GET MORE SUPPORT THAN YOU DESERVE

. . . .

You will need: no conscience

. . . .

Call up a help line and invent a trauma. If you've just been dumped by a man you knew for a week, tell them that your husband of ten years just died. If you've gained weight, tell them that you've got a tumor the size of Washington and can't get out of your house for surgery. If you're merely bored, tell them that your problem isn't unique—is it? Have they heard any good ones that evening?

☼ ☼ ☼ LEISURE ☼ ☼ ☼

Impress Your Boss

You will need: a cast for your ankle

Tell your boss that you love riding, playing polo, or any dangerous sport. Invite him to take part with you. The morning of the big day, strap on your ankle cast and appear with a tear-stained face. "It hurts so much," you say bravely. "But I am willing to try it anyway. I hope I don't let you down!" Your boss will be very, very impressed. . . .

Be a Buffet Philosopher

You will need: a lunch counter

Stand at the lunch counter with your plate and gaze over the various dishes. Call the "chef" over for a short chat. "Is this a salad?" you ask, pointing to a Jell-O dish with marshmallows. "Because this doesn't look anything like that green mix of leaves over there," you say as you gesture to the bowl of arugula no one has touched. Get them to define what they mean by a salad until they either strike you or ask you to leave. Then sue them.

Make a Little Extra Money

. . . .

You will need: clown makeup and a car

. . . .

Show up at your local airport dressed as a clown. Put one small wheel on your car and paint the vehicle wacky colors. Pick up passengers by beating off other legitimate taxis with squirts from your lapel daisy and loud honks from your clown horn. When you drop them off at the wrong location, say, "I'm a clown! What did you expect? Look at the slogan on the car: 'Laughing on the outside, no insurance on the inside!'"

☼ ☼ ☼ **LEISURE** ☼ ☼ ☼

Be a County Fair Innovator

You will need: your own county fair

If you can't win at your local county fair, open your own. Include all the things that a normal county fair wouldn't dare to have. Have a casino that uses real odds and real money and has real gangsters if you don't pay up. (If challenged, insist you have Native blood.) Hire a geek to bite the heads off chickens. Invite his family, too, and let them drink.

✳ ✳ ✳ LEISURE ✳ ✳ ✳

Dump a Sensitive Man

....

You will need: a deep dark secret
(fake, of course)

....

Call your boyfriend. Tell him that there's no point in being
cruel when all you have to say is the truth: being with him
has made you feel brave enough to face your fears. Yes,
that's right. You are not only going to have a sex change,
but you are also going to become celibate until it's been
done. Add that it's all thanks to him and
would he like to come to the Good-Bye,
Cruel World Awards ceremony—tickets are
only $50?

♥♥♥ ROMANCE ♥♥♥

Drag a Date

....

You will need: a lifeguard swimsuit, a whistle, and one of those orange/red floaty things you see on *Baywatch*

....

Remember how everyone says there are plenty more fish in the sea? Catch your own date by pretending to be a lifeguard. Stroll around the beach (staying away from the real lifeguard station), keeping your posture upright. The minute someone you like goes into the water, look around and yell, "I'm on it!" and "I've got you!" Drag the one you like out of the water. It's a great way to break the ice.

♥♥♥ ROMANCE ♥♥♥

Be a Therapy Expert

You will need: someone you want to teach a lesson to

Tell your colleagues that controlling one's emotions is vital. "You must subsume, contain, and control anger. If you must, clench your fists, grind your teeth, or get an ulcer, but do not allow, under any circumstances, your emotions to get the upper hand." Carry on, getting angrier as you do. Finally, turn and leave, slamming the door on your way out.

➤ ➤ ➤ OFFICE ➤ ➤ ➤

Start a Petition

You will need: a long piece of paper and several pens

No way does your workplace have a suite of showers, day care, or a sauna. Yet it's every American's right to access all those services at work. Start a petition for management to install them all. Write down a few fictitious names to get the ball rolling. Do not sign your own name; make sure your bête noire signs first.

●●● OFFICE ●●●

HAVE THE BEST VACATION, EVER

· ·

You will need: language tapes, brochures, books about your destination

· ·

Get all information about your vacation destination some months in advance and get your partner to study the tapes and gather information on the locals. Then book somewhere else entirely where the language is English and the lore is nonexistent. Excuse yourself by saying, "The country was booked solid."

☼ ☼ ☼ LEISURE ☼ ☼ ☼

HOST A BAD BBQ

. . . .

You will need: creepy meat

. . . .

Have a BBQ party at night. Load the grill with offal,
liver, and maybe a few bits of meat that are past their
sell-by date. Throw things on the grill that will fall
through. Burn the stuff that other people bring. Feed
vegetarians real meat. Make carnivores eat tofu.

✵ ✵ ✵ LEISURE ✵ ✵ ✵

Day 221

Be a Big Baseball Fan

....

You will need: big hats, big sponge hands, hot dogs, peanuts, popcorn, etc.

....

Sit down in the stands, looking really intense and professional. Get yourself set with the cards and the radio earpiece plug-in so you can follow the game over the airwaves. Wear a hat. Then, just as the game gets going, turn to a rabid, transfixed fan and ask, "So, who's playing? Are they winning yet? When's the thing going to end?"

☙☙☙ **MISCHIEF** ☙☙☙

Use the Airport Cart

. . . .

You will need: a bit of duct tape and a safety pin

. . . .

Why let only the elderly, infirm, and truly needy use those handy airport carts? Get to your gate fast by taping up your leg and pinning any excess fabric. You'll soon be on one of those motorized beauties. Let your leg down only when you get seated in first class.

Fight Unwanted Holiday Snaps

You will need: pictures of monkeys, your rear end, etc.

Bothered by coworkers who send out mass e-mails with their holiday snaps? Get your revenge by "accidentally" sending out your own holiday snaps. Instead of beautiful children, girlfriends, and sunsets, your photos will be of repulsive and puzzling monkeys, your butt, drunk fat naked guys, and many shots of the floor or ceiling. Those happy snappy e-mails will cease, guaranteed.

OFFICE

Explain DIY Liposuction

You will need: duct tape

Explain to a lard-ass coworker that they don't have to give up beer and fried food. Tell them not to eat for a day at least. On the morning of the second day, get them to lean forward and suck in their stomach. As the stomach goes in, grab the tape and put a large cross of strong tape across the inward-headed stomach. Sure, it will hurt, but boy, it sure looks good—and it's so much cheaper than liposuction.

Get That Convertible You Always Wanted

. . . .

You will need: a very low bridge

. . . .

Buy a really cheap car. Find a low bridge and drive the car underneath it, scraping off the roof of the car. Duck down low but keep speed to about 15 mph to get the desired "convertible" effect. Okay, so you'll not have the windshield either, but you can enjoy driving it around for a few days before the police impound the car and slam you in jail.

☼☼☼ **LEISURE** ☼☼☼

Be a Poignant Device

You will need: nonwaterproof mascara,
blush, and balled-up tissues

Set other people's nerves on edge by weeping in
public. Not only does this make other people pay
attention to you, wonder about you, and want to buy
you things, it also makes them feel much better about
their own lives. N.B. Make sure to reapply blush if
your eyes are not red enough.

☼ ☼ ☼ LEISURE ☼ ☼ ☼

Day 227

Be Popular with Airport Security

....

You will need: a skeleton and a golf/ski bag

....

Buy a medical-standard skeleton and pack it into your ski or golf bag. Take the bag through the X-ray machine and just watch the security people's faces light up with excitement and merriment. It beats trying to take a firearm through the X-ray machine any day.

🕭 🕭 🕭 **MISCHIEF** 🕭 🕭 🕭

Make Your Own Bug Remedy

....

You will need: a neighbor troubled by flies or mosquitos

....

Flies and bugs can be a real menace. If you have a neighbor who is very troubled by wasps and such, offer your own traditional remedy for a bug-free life: the honey trap. Put some honey, heavily sugared water, or syrup into a jar. The bugs will be attracted to that jar. Placement of the jar is vital: inside the house is best, although near the clothesline or swimming pool is also good.

🎇 🎇 🎇 MISCHIEF 🎇 🎇 🎇

GET SPECIAL AIRPORT TREATMENT

. . . .

You will need: a pair of glam sunglasses; to call the airline before you go

. . . .

Call the airline and say that you are really ill. Say you'll need help getting to the gate, help with your baggage, and help basically doing anything. Then show up at the airport looking great and say, "I'm having a good day today. But tomorrow, you'll never know. In fact, I could drop at any moment." Swan through the airport wearing your sunglasses as if you were a Hollywood star.

☼ ☼ ☼ LEISURE ☼ ☼ ☼

Day 230

MAKE FRIENDS ON A FLIGHT

· ·

You will need: a list of the films shown
during your flight

· ·

Most films on flights are edited for violence and sex.
But you can make friends immediately by filling in
those details in a loud voice during the film so everyone
can hear. Also, you can put in the real swear words to
enhance the excitement of the adventure scenes: "It's a
real f***ing gun, not a real fudging gun!"

☼☼☼ LEISURE ☼☼☼

Psyche Out a Competitive Coworker

You will need: to have a beach about four hours from your work

Put sand in your shoes at work, put some weeds in your hair and a bit of blush on your cheekbones and nose. Come in pretending to have been at the beach before work. "There's nothing like the beach in the morning," you say, stretching healthily. Take work home to get ahead, but make the whole workday look effortless.

● ● ● OFFICE ● ● ●

Set Up a Lemonade Stand

You will need:

a homemade-lemonade stand

Nothing says innocence and childhood more than a homemade-lemonade stand, so set one up in the office parking lot at lunchtime. Make it extremely popular by serving just the right lemonade—not too sweet, not too sour—in charming recyclable cups. With a big shot of booze in it.

● ● ● OFFICE ● ● ●

Scare Some Kids

....

You will need: black paint, glue, and scary
animal bones

....

There's nothing worse than happily
playing children if you're not in the mood for
their joy, especially if they haven't the skills to keep
their toys from coming into your personal space. So,
when anything comes your way, grab it. Paint it black
and throw it back to them. Or glue chicken
bones all over it. Or puncture it.

☺ ☺ ☹ FAMILY ☺ ☺ ☹

Help Kids from Overdeveloped Nations

You will need: to be a camp counselor

Take a niece or nephew to fat camp.
They really help overweight kids, and being a
fat-camp counselor helps you, too. Put to use all that
hectoring that your mother tried on you during your
formative years. Remember "Oh you're doing so well
but MY LORD LOOK AT YOUR THIGHS!"? Just as
effective today as it was then.

☺ ☺ ☹ FAMILY ☺ ☺ ☹

Encourage a Marathon Runner

·······················

You will need: a car with bad emissions

Find a runner. Marathon running takes a lot of practice but you, too, can be of enormous assistance. There's nothing like a pep talk while someone is running to lift their spirits and maybe improve their time. Drive your smoking, spluttering car next to a runner. Drive along chatting with them until they turn blue.

🐞🐞🐞 MISCHIEF 🐞🐞🐞

Play with In-line Skaters

....

You will need: some sticks and a dog
on a leash

....

There's always a spot in the park where the skaters go

to practice. Find their most dangerous, threatening

curve and set up camp with your dog. Keeping the dog

on the leash, sit in the shade and wait until the skaters

are almost to the curve. Throw sticks into their path.

Watch that dog go!

💣💣💣 MISCHIEF 💣💣💣

Bring the Beach to Work

You will need: some sand, a bucket, a seagull

Can't get to the beach? Order a ton of sand (easily found at your local builder's merchant), a child's beach bucket, and shovel to be delivered to the office parking lot. A recording of waves played on the car stereo will complete the scene. Put your towel in the best spot.

Get Sympathy

You will need: a lot of blush

Brush or slather blush all over your shoulders, nose, forehead, back, and chest. Put blush on your knees and leave some un-blushed tracks where your clothes would have been. Go to work wearing very light clothing; sit down lightly and flinch at anything that may get near you. Yell, "Don't touch me!" whenever anyone goes near you.

◆◆◆ OFFICE ◆◆◆

Throw a Great Outdoor Party

....

You will need: a backyard

....

Throw a 1950s party. Give everyone a drink as they enter your house—"Hey, Bill, what's your poison?" Half an hour later, shove everyone into the backyard with the words, "It's the warmest night of the year!" whether it is or not. Let them have fun on their own with just people and a drink, like the old days. Don't forget to put one or two dangerous tiki torches way in the corner where they will offer no light or heat.

✿ ✿ ✿ LEISURE ✿ ✿ ✿

Get a Good Airline Seat

....

You will need: a portable DVD player

....

Airline films can be extremely tedious, so bring along your own set of DVDs that would otherwise be banned onboard. Anything with a plane crash, pornography, or loud explosions will make those seated next to you demand another seat. If all else fails, bring a DVD of a loudly crying baby—it is the next best thing to actually having one.

☼ ☼ ☼ LEISURE ☼ ☼ ☼

SCARE SOME KIDS AGAIN

You will need: scary German mint candies,
a gray wig, and a brown paper bag

Are the kids driving
you mad with their happy play and
tinkling voices? Scare them off by appearing at
the door of their room in a gray wig. Hold a brown
paper bag filled with creepy German candies. Yell
loudly, "Von't you komm in for mein candies?" and
see how many take up your offer.

☺ ☺ ☹ FAMILY ☺ ☺ ☹

CLOSE THE AIRSPACE

You will need: a microwave oven

If it isn't baseballs and
basketballs and skateboards, it's
the errant Frisbee that occasionally requires
special treatment. Take the Frisbee and microwave it
until it reaches an unrecognizable shape. Walk it
back to the perpetrator and hand it over to them.
Apologize for its altered, wizened shape by
explaining, "I washed it and it wouldn't dry!"

☺ ☺ ☹ FAMILY ☺ ☺ ☹

WIN AT THE FAIR

. . . .

You will need: pals with large wads of cash

. . . .

Amusement parks are the new in thing. So impress your
wealthy friends with your stunning ability to win a big
teddy bear, an inflatable dog, and a half-dead fish by
getting them to pay for you to shoot at something or
throw a rock at a coconut. Actually, usually just paying
the entrance fee gets you a prize, but you want the BIG
one. Scream and stamp your feet if a booth owner won't
let you win what you want.

☼ ☼ ☼ LEISURE ☼ ☼ ☼

GET SOME RESPECT

....

You will need: a cute bike

....

Sure, your bicycle is cute, but no one really respects it,
especially the mountain bike fraternity that sometimes
won't even move out of the way when you cycle past.
Make them notice you by mounting a deafeningly loud
truck horn on your handlebars. Paint it the same
color as your bike and use it when you are extremely
near other cyclists.

☼ ☼ ☼ LEISURE ☼ ☼ ☼

Make Your Boss Respect You

You will need: a fraidy-cat boss

Everyone's got something to hide, and the higher up the corporate ladder they go, the more there is to hide. So search local court offices for judgments against your boss. Drunk driving, sexual assault, bankruptcy, and nonpayment of alimony are all good things to know about them. And then let them know that you know.

Help a Fat Friend

You will need: an afternoon off work to shop and eat

You can help anyone lose weight by being an example of how fun it is to not be fat. Take your favorite fat coworker out for a day of shopping for bikinis and lingerie: make sure you are together in the dressing room to be each other's morale booster. Say, "Oh, heavens, look at my thighs!" and ask her, "Honestly, do I look heavy in this?" Afterward, go for a big piece of cake and a cup of hot chocolate with whipped cream on top. She'll be in tears of gratitude.

Shop with a Pal

....

You will need: a poker face

....

One must never offend a friend. So what if the clothes she buys make her look like the back end of a bus? It's not your job to tell her so. Take her shopping and try to teach her some sense of aesthetics by offering her clothing that definitely looks awful on her. If she likes it, she'll love your taste. And if she doesn't, you'll be training her sense of chic slowly but surely. Either way, she'll look like a fool. But you're still her friend!

❧ ❧ ❧ MISCHIEF ❧ ❧ ❧

Day 248

Be an Editor

....

You will need: some web-design skills and a
slew of e-mail addresses

....

Create your own online magazine. You can make it
as sassy or classy as you like—and you never know,
even an oddball interest can take off—but make sure
that all the people you hate get thoroughly roasted
in it. You may even end up selling your opinion-zine
about potatoes, called "The Tater," for millions of
dollars. It could happen.

🎳 🎳 🎳 MISCHIEF 🎳 🎳 🎳

SHE BUYS IT, YOU WEAR IT

....

You will need: a sister with a lot of unmaxed credit cards

....

There's nothing quite like a sister who allows you to borrow her clothes and shoes and coats and maybe even cars and boyfriends. Encourage her to spend as much as possible on beautiful designer wear, then borrow it before it gets stained, shapeless, or out of fashion. Every time you see her, remind her that you have her clothing. This makes you look honest and merely forgetful.

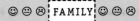 ☺ ☹ ☺ FAMILY ☺ ☹ ☺

LOVE HER, HATE HIM

· ·

You will need: a will of iron

· ·

What to do when a sister takes up with a hound of a man?
You can't tell her that he's no good for her. That will only
make her want him more. You must, although it may hurt
you, do the opposite. Go overboard. Say that he's
wonderful, he's sensational, that he invented aspirin and
showed you his war wound, which is in a very interesting
place. Say that you also saw him chewing his own toenails,
and that's quite a skill. She'll soon get the message and
you'll look innocent.

☺ ☺ ☹ 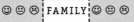 FAMILY ☺ ☺ ☹

Play with the New Arrival

You will need: a new underling at the office

Whenever someone new starts at the office, they need a bit of hazing to really let them know that they've been accepted. Make sure that you sit next to them at the first meeting of the day. After fifteen minutes, jump out of your chair holding your crotch and yell, "Hey, man, what the heck?!"

● ● ● OFFICE ● ● ●

Day 252

Get to Know Your Boss

You will need: access to his office

Check his garbage when he's out of the office and
then check his home garbage, too. The things that
he throws away will amaze you. Find out
what high school he attended and call a few
of his old school buddies. Pump them for
embarrassing stories about your boss—tell them
it's for a testimonial dinner. Start dropping hints
that you know about those long-ago events and
watch him squirm. See? Knowledge is power.

●●● OFFICE ●●●

Date a Friend's Boyfriend on the Sly

. . . .

You will need: a heart of stone and nerves of steel

. . . .

Some friends are merely acquaintances. This is what you will tell yourself as you seduce a friend's boyfriend. Other excuses you can use are "If he loved her so much, why would he cheat on her with me?" and "Surely she knows what's going on and approves, otherwise she would say something." Either way, this is the man's fault: if he could control himself, so could you.

♥ ♥ ♥ ROMANCE ♥ ♥ ♥

Stop Your Man Fawning Over His Ex

....

You will need: some quality time with HER

....

Have your man invite his ex out for a drink to meet you.
When he goes to get the drinks or talks to someone else,
ask her, "How are the hemorrhoids? I understand you had a
terrible body hair problem; he was saying that you
probably have that all taken care of now. . ." By the time
he comes back for a chat, she will be angry and upset. She
will not speak to him ever again either.

♥♥♥ ROMANCE ♥♥♥

Feed a Vegetarian

....

You will need: hard bits of vegetables and lots of cheese

....

Invite a vegetarian friend to dinner and fix them a healthy, body-respecting plate of broccoli stalks, bean stalks, and other items that people normally throw out. Nothing says "good for you" more than a sheet of cabbage too tough to cut with a normal knife. Cover everything in cheese and serve: remember, few vegetarians can eat all that cow food without the addition of our friend, Mr. Queso.

🎇 🎇 🎇 MISCHIEF 🎇 🎇 🎇

Make Spring Cleaning Easy

·························

You will need: the classifieds

·························

Although you can't remember when you last did it, you
forgot to spring clean the house again. This means that the
windows are barely transparent, the carpeting looks like a
field of marbles, and the parquet floor looks as if it has
been carpeted. So, it is time to "spring clean." Find
another apartment and move into it immediately.

Smoke Out the Office Thief

You will need: access to the guilty party's desk and a ton of office stationery

There's nothing like a new person on the team to make one's mind think laterally. If someone new is threatening your office security, get them fired for theft by hiding stationery in their desk. Make sure there aren't any security cameras watching and that you wear CSI-style rubber gloves to prevent any possible DNA transfer from you onto said stolen papyrus. Look sympathetic when they are discovered and make a lot of tutting noises.

Be a Makeup Artist

You will need: anyone at work

At lunchtime, take a coworker to a large makeup counter and get a makeover from one of the cheapest brands they have. Ask for a "full evening face" for her, while you opt for "natural and hypoallergenic" makeup. Afterward, get her to walk around the bad part of town without cleaning any of the makeup off.

That will be interesting.

Look Great in Your Sister's Company

....

You will need: a really odd shade of lipstick

....

Arrange a date with the sister who looks marginally better than you, and on meeting insist that she tries "this year's European sensation in lipstick"—which is any horrid lipstick you manage to find in the sales bin. She'll be more clown than pretty.

☺ ☺ ☹ FAMILY ☺ ☺ ☹

Undermine Your Brother

. . . .

You will need: photos of your father's friends

. . . .

Get a whole heap of photos of your father's friends. Study them with your brother, then step back. Hold one up to his face and say, "Hey! You look a lot like Barry!" Look at him as if to say, "All these years I thought we were blood. . . ." Next year, send him a formal birthday and Christmas card as if he were a stranger.

☺ ☺ ☹ **FAMILY** ☺ ☺ ☹

Keep Track of Your Man

....

You will need: a small but loud bell

....

Men wander. Sometimes you can't even find them in the house. Keep track of your man the easy way by putting a small bell on his zipper. This way you can tell where he is and what he's doing every minute of the day—without shelling out a lot of money for fancy tracking technology.

♥♥♥ ROMANCE ♥♥♥

Make Time for Love

....

You will need: innovative hiding places

....

Get extra time with your boyfriend by sabotaging his shoelaces (putting small nicks in them so they break the minute he tries to tie them). Go even further by hiding his pants, his underwear, and even his shoes. Nothing says "I love you" as much as, "Where the heck are my clothes?" when uttered by a man with an angry throbbing vein on his forehead.

♥ ♥ ♥ ROMANCE ♥ ♥ ♥

Help the Lady Next Door

....

You will need: a bunch of spiders or
other insects

....

The lady next door hasn't been outside her house for
weeks. Why not help her get some fresh air by putting
a large number of spiders or crickets through her
mail slot? She will think it is a biblical story come
true and flee her abode. Screaming and running
into the fresh air is such a good way to lift
a shut-in's spirits.

❀ ❀ ❀ ETIQUETTE ❀ ❀ ❀

Get a Tan for Free!

....

You will need: a nice newsstand where they
don't bother you

....

Want nice tanned legs but haven't seen the sun for weeks?
Never fear. Go to your nearest newsstand and go through
all the women's magazines. Take out at least twenty
packets of foundation samples from the pages. Take
them home and apply them to your legs: everyone knows
that foundation samples in magazines are always the
right shade—for legs.

❀ ❀ ❀ ETIQUETTE ❀ ❀ ❀

Have Wrong-Number Fun

. . . .

You will need: a phone number similar to a restaurant's

Whenever someone calls you to make a reservation for a restaurant that has a telephone number like yours, take the reservation. Make it realistic: Smoking? Outside? Would you like to leave a contact number and credit card? Soon, the restaurant will go bust or change its number.

🎆 🎆 🎆 MISCHIEF 🎆 🎆 🎆

Cause a Catfight

....

You will need: two e-mails and everyone's
e-mail address

....

Are your friends getting together and not inviting you?

Break up their happy camp with a flurry of insulting,

obscene e-mails claiming to be from one friend to

another, saying one is a cow and vice versa. The risk is

that they discover that these e-mails are all a fraud

(and even worse, from you) but at best this will make

them deeply distrust each other and

turn to you for advice.

💣 💣 💣 **MISCHIEF** 💣 💣 💣

Start a Rumor

You will need: a believable face

How much does anyone know about the people who own the company that you work for? So start a rumor. They dress all in black and drive red Fords, and none of them look like a man or a woman, but both. They're triplets who own an island on which there's a lab dedicated to transplanting human heads. See how long it takes for one of your rumors to come back to you.

●●● OFFICE ●●●

Turn Your Rival into the Office "Girl"

You will need: someone in the office who really annoys you

Encourage your office rival to sleep with—or at least try to seduce—everyone in the office, bar no one. Tell her/him that "this company has a dirty secret—everyone sleeps with everyone else and it's all down to promotions for sex." If they try to discuss this with anyone, they'll look very odd indeed. If they mention your name, it will look even worse for them. If they follow your advice, tell human resources all about it.

●━━● ● OFFICE ● ●━━●

BE A HUMBLE DINER

....

You will need: an envelope filled with
a moderate amount of change

....

Avoid paying for meals by being the ideal
restaurant patron—you're very kind and pleasant
to the waiter, you talk to the owner and the
chef, laugh at their jokes—and then, at the end
of the meal, produce an envelope instead of a
wallet. Mutter something like, "I can't believe
this is all I had. I was sure I had more," while
taking out pennies one at a time until someone
offers to pay your bill out of sheer frustration.

❀ ❀ ❀ ETIQUETTE ❀ ❀ ❀

BE THE DEVIL'S AVOCADO

....

You will need: a big mouth

....

Sick of hearing about how good a certain diet is? Tired of hearing about how eating only eggs and gravel works wonders for your figure? Then do something about it by pointing out the problems with any diet approach: high protein damages the kidneys; low fat will make you hungry for weeks; high carbohydrate can lead to type 2 diabetes.

❀❀❀ ETIQUETTE ❀❀❀

BE THE FAMILY FAVORITE

You will need: lots of truly shocking e-mails

Break into your
siblings' e-mail accounts and send
the worst e-mails you can find from their
accounts to yours—pornography, spam, chain
letters, etc. Wait until you have a good packet of
offensive e-mails, then print them out and show
them all to your parents, saying, "Look at all this!
How can you have raised them to hate me so
much?"

☺ ☺ ☹ FAMILY ☺ ☺ ☹

GET A NEW APARTMENT

You will need: access to a truly horrible apartment

Throw a party at the
nastiest and ugliest and, possibly,
smelliest apartment you can find. Invite your
parents. Make everything else absolutely perfect:
drink, food, company, service. Pretend that the
apartment is yours. Your parents will so hate "your"
place that they'll pay the deposit and first three
months' rent on a new one.

☺ ☻ ☹ FAMILY ☺ ☻ ☹

Impress Your Friends

....

You will need: a good eye for celebrities

....

Impress your friends by walking up to any celebrity you
see at a restaurant or bar or party. Poke them in the chest
with your finger and ask, "Hey, how's Jack? How's
Leonardo? How's Madonna?" If the famous face strikes you,
sets their bodyguard on you, or flees, turn to your friends
and make the "What happened there?" gesture with a
shoulder shrug and grimace. Walk back to your friends and
say, "Celebrities are so high-strung!"

❧ ❧ ❧ **MISCHIEF** ❧ ❧ ❧

Day 274

Name a Baby

· ·

You will need: a chemical imbalance in your brain

· ·

Befriend your nearest and dearest single mom. Start
talking about names with her early on. Warm her up to the
idea that naming her child "Yoda" or "Darth" would be a
very good idea, seeing as it would give the child an instant
"in" with friends and their parents.

DESIGN A DRESS
FOR YOUR SISTER

....

**You will need: some old dress of your sister's
that you hate and a handful of safety pins**

....

Take your sister's dress that you hate and be innovative

with safety pins. Make the dress shorter, lopsided

("asymmetrical"), or tear it and pin it together to make it

punk. The best thing here is that by altering the dress

with pins, you will more than likely ruin the dress to the

point where she'll have to get rid of it and get a new one.

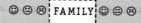

☺ ☺ ☹ FAMILY ☺ ☺ ☹

GET THE HOUSE

·························

You will need: a couple of dented walkers and bruises on your body

·························

Are your parents being unreasonable? Play football and get some bruises on your body. Then call the authorities and say that your 75-year-old parents are beating you with their walkers and you have the physical proof. Few authorities will believe your parents, especially with their fingerprints all over the walkers and you with matching bruises.

☺ 😐 ☹ FAMILY ☺ 😐 ☹

Label His Car

....

You will need: bumper stickers you
make yourself

....

Why not doctor your ex-boyfriend's car—and warn other
potential dates at the same time—with your own bespoke
bumper stickers? If he drives a sports car, label it, "Yes,
it is true what they say about men who drive sports cars"
or "My other car gave someone tetanus." Make the
sticker as readable as possible and use
the correct, unremovable glue, too.

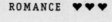

♥ ♥ ♥ ROMANCE ♥ ♥ ♥

Get Out of Making Dinner

....

You will need: a sedative and up-to-date
home insurance

....

Invite a man over for dinner. Take the sedative so that you
collapse seconds after he comes in. By the time you wake
up, he should have made dinner for you both AND you
won't be asked for sex later. If it goes wrong and your
apartment has been emptied of its contents, remember not
to pick up guys in that bar again. Make your insurance
claim and dream about your new interior. . . .

♥♥♥ ROMANCE ♥♥♥

Quell a Blond Rival

You will need: an empty bottle of household bleach

Wait until she has alluded to her natural blonditude, say, five times, and then "pick up" the empty bottle of bleach from under your desk. Ask, "Did this drop out of your bag? I'm a fake brunette."

Get the Afternoon Off

You will need: a tub of yogurt

Eat lunch at your desk and type away as you munch a sandwich. Look very busy, too busy to stop for a moment. After the sandwich, open the yogurt with a sharp tug. Make sure that you spill all of the yogurt onto your keyboard. Dab at the mess, scream, and smear yogurt on your face, making your mascara run. Become demented at having "lost all that work." You'll need time off to recover.

● ● ● OFFICE ● ● ●

Divorce Down the Middle

....

You will need: a chain saw

....

Breaking up is hard to do, but you can make it easier by being reasonable. And fair is as fair does: he gets half and you get half. So, once you've agreed to a civil breakup, start the proceedings by sawing everything in half—kitchen table, chairs, sofa. He'll start accepting your demands soon enough.

☺ ☺ ☹ FAMILY ☺ ☺ ☹

Distress the Family

. . . .

You will need: Turkey Day smarts

. . . .

Prepare a special Thanksgiving Quiz. Questions
include, "When did we first celebrate Thanksgiving?"
"What is it for?" "Why do we eat turkey?" Watch the
family sweat as they realize they know nothing.

☺ ☻ ☹ FAMILY ☺ ☻ ☹

Vacation in Florida

....

You will need: a boyfriend with money

....

Tell your true love that you love fall—the cold, the damp, the disease. You love the fact that you can get fat, your body shape hidden under copious, unsexy sweaters and ugly boots with leggings. You adore the change in season because it means you'll stop walking completely, taking cabs and private limos for the rest of the year. You also suffer from SAD, which turns you into a complete bitch by January. You'll be wintering in Florida in no time.

♥♥♥   ROMANCE   ♥♥♥

Day 284

Make a Sexy Man
Feel Hideous

....

You will need: to look ugly in the face

....

If by some fluke a good-looking guy rejects you,
immediately call an ugly agency and start serially
dating the facially challenged. After your third date with
an extra from *Freaks*, the looker will start to feel that his
regular features, conventional so-called beauty, and dull
symmetry are the reason you don't want to date him.

He is yours now, so reject him.

♥♥♥   ROMANCE   ♥♥♥

Freak Out a Steak House

....

You will need: to not be that hungry

....

Go to a steak house and get really fussy about your food. What cow is it from? What color is the cow? Did it have a name? Can you see photos of its parents? After you've made your choice, start asking for a weird way of having the meat prepared: blue with some red and then the other bits black. Send it back if it is not right.

❧ ❧ ❧ **MISCHIEF** ❧ ❧ ❧

Do as the Romans Do

....

You will need: a cast-iron stomach

....

Every time you travel, make it a point to order the local delicacy, whatever it is—only get your partner or traveling companion to eat it while you take the credit. "Yes, I ate Chihuahua in Korea," you can exclaim while your partner had to spend two weeks in the hospital getting over the cramps.

🝔 🝔 🝔 **MISCHIEF** 🝔 🝔 🝔

Quell a Blond Rival: 2

You will need: a sharp, cutting voice

We all know blondes have more fun, but they can also cause more pain than other hair colors, particularly when they lie about how they get their golden tresses. This goes double for your rival, who crows on and on about her natural hair. Whenever she mentions, as she will, her platinum locks, say in a low but loud voice, "Three words. Collar and cuffs."

Get a Few Days Off Work

You will need: to use shock tactic

Do not comb or wash your hair. Apply makeup haphazardly. Once at work, sit still for an hour, doing nothing. Then jump up wildly, scream, and stab yourself in the chest just where you have cunningly put a "squib" of fake blood (the blood packs they use in the movies). One look at that spurting fountain from your chest and you'll be whisked out of the office PDQ. Bribe the ambulance driver and take a few days off work.

●●● OFFICE ●●●

Day 289

APPRAISE
FAMILY LIFE

....

You will need: a fantastic single person's pad

....

Feeling the pressure that you don't have a family, have no children, and are not married? Feel better instantly by comparing happy, bustling family homes with your empty bachelorette apartment. Point out that you have more stuff, money, and taste. Make your sibling feel like a country cousin who smells of baby wee and who will never be able to wear a sheath dress again—you win!

☺ ☷ ☹ 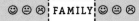 FAMILY ☺ ☷ ☹

Day 290

LEARN TO KNIT

....

You will need: knitting needles, wool, and no idea whatsoever

....

Now's the time to start bitching while you stitch. Knitting is fun and you can make your family gifts, too. Nothing says "I Love You" better than something made by hand. Learn to knit by rubbing the knitting needles together until they spark. The flames may catch the eye of someone who actually can knit and they will come over, put out the fire, and show you how to thread your wool onto the pointy parts of the needle. Remember, if you don't recognize what you've knitted, say it is modern art.

 ☺ ☺ ☹ FAMILY ☺ ☺ ☹

Make Money from the Theater

....

You will need: a theater, some players, and maybe an audience

....

Write a play about what has happened in your love life and threaten to put it on at the nearest theater. Get an interview with you in the local paper telling all about it. Get your photo in the paper. Call it "Sizable Matters." Your former lovers will undoubtedly pay you not to stage what would be a very expensive production.

♥♥♥ ROMANCE ♥♥♥

Turn Him Off

. . . .

You will need: anything that is visually
offensive to your man

. . . .

Don't want to have sex tonight? Want your man to leave
you alone? Remember that men, being visually oriented,
are easily put off by anything that smacks of practicality.
Tucking your shirt into your pantyhose, wearing a
maternity or sports bra, or even wearing short socks and
not shaving your legs should send the appropriate "not
tonight" signals his way.

♥♥♥ ROMANCE ♥♥♥

Stop That Lovin' Feeling

You will need: a couple of people at work who really annoy you

Mention in passing to the office gossip that you think that the two people you most dislike are having an affair. Say that you could have sworn you saw them sneaking into a bar together, or out of a hotel in the afternoon. Doesn't matter if they're the same sex. People might hate and fear you, but you'll be filed under "Always knows what's going on" in their minds.

A promotion is sure to follow.

●●● OFFICE ●●●

Get Them Fired

You will need: a few minutes with the boss

Once the rumor has started, it won't be long before those two office workers have an illicit romance. So tell on them. Telling the boss will be for their own good. "Our fearless leader was beginning to get suspicious," you say in your defense—if you can be bothered defending yourself.

●●● OFFICE ●●●

Day 295

GET A FREE HOLIDAY

. . . .

You will need: a good sense of geography

. . . .

Go to a chat room of your choice and find someone you can stand to talk to from the area of the world you want to visit. After a few weeks, you can get yourself invited to their area—hopefully, a tropical paradise— and stay with them for free! Get the airfare included by pretending that your parents won't pay for it.

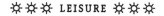

☼ ☼ ☼ LEISURE ☼ ☼ ☼

GET A DECENT MEAL

....

You will need: very fancy tastes

....

At the airport, ask for the "religious difference" meal.
When they say they don't have it, call them unbelievers
and pagans. When they sigh and ask what you want,
give them a list of your requirements, pointing out that
there's still time for someone to get you some beluga
caviar and Cristal champagne from the airport shop.

☼☼☼ LEISURE ☼☼☼

Don't Talk with Your Mouth Full

. . . .

You will need: food in front of you

. . . .

A true lady never speaks with food in her mouth, and you
are a true lady, which is why some rich man is going to
take you to dinner—just ask one, he'll say yes. Since you
want to have fun with this guy, do not put any food in
your mouth while he's talking, but only when he pauses
for you to speak. Eat well and don't speak until the meal is
over. Then say, "Thank you."

❀ ❀ ❀ ETIQUETTE ❀ ❀ ❀

Free Willy

· ·

You will need: insider knowledge of the fish world

· ·

Fish are an endangered species, you know, so when anyone orders it within your earshot, make it very plain you disapprove by yelling, "Not that! That's almost extinct, you know! Oh, not mahimahi! Do you know there are only a thousand of them left in captivity?" Finally allow them to order the farmed salmon that swims in its own wee: that, at least, is environmentally sound. For somebody.

❀ ❀ ❀ ETIQUETTE ❀ ❀ ❀

Day 299

Get Free Meals for a Month

· ·

You will need: a cockroach

Keep a recently deceased and unsquashed cockroach in
your purse. Go to a good (but not local) restaurant and
order food that has a sauce of some kind. Eat half and then
slip the cockroach into the sauce. Scream loudly when you
pull it out of your food. The more hysterical you can be,
the more chance that you'll get some compensation from
the owners. Ask for at least a month of lunches or
you'll tell the city health inspectors.

Guess This Mess

....

**You will need: that special casserole recipe
of your grandmother's**

....

Love your friends but hate entertaining? Have them over
but serve "the family special"—a casserole so disgustingly
ugly that no one can speak once the lid is taken off the
pot. Be ready for this to happen by having a pizza delivery
number at hand. You'll never be asked to cook again.

💣 💣 💣 MISCHIEF 💣 💣 💣

Nerds Don't Date

You will need: a computer that breaks easily

There's always some IT nerd who thinks that you fancy him. So encourage him by flirting all day and then, when he comes loping around toward the end of the day, point him out to someone and say loudly: "He taught me that WWW doesn't just mean World Wide Web—it also means Wee Willy Winky."

●►● OFFICE ●►●

Fix That Photo

You will need: an IT colleague who thinks you're cute

Once you've mastered the art of making two images look like one (ask the IT nerd how), gather images of coworkers or the boss and create new artwork with them. You could gather images from interesting websites—perhaps the ones that advertise larger penises, for instance— and insert your friends into them.

●●● OFFICE ●●●

UPSET THE YOUNG

You will need: some traditional children's books

If pressed by annoying
nephews and nieces to read them
some bedtime garbage they love, do so with a
smile, but on the last page say, "And then what
happened?" The tot will obligingly pipe up, "And
they all lived happily after." This is when you frown
and say, "No. It says here that they all went to jail,
where they rotted."

☺ ☺ ☹ FAMILY ☺ ☺ ☹

MAKE YOUR HOME A NO-GO ZONE

You will need: nothing but turkey

For the sport of it,
invite all your irritating and
braying relatives over for dinner. Make
everything—from starter to dessert—out of turkey.
Serve turkey juice to drink, turkey rice pudding for
dessert, turkey-stuffed cabbage for a side dish, and
turkey mole fudge brownies for afterward with
turkey-flavored coffee. They will never come again
no matter how much you beg.

☺ ☺ ☹ FAMILY ☺ ☺ ☹

Babysit Your Favorite Nephew: 3

· ·

**You will need: uncut DVD versions of *Halloween*
and *I Know What You Did Last Summer***

· ·

Persuade your sibling that you want to babysit the
nephew you've always hated because you need to get to
know each other. Take along candy and a horror mask
for him. Keep the DVDs hidden until his parents have
left. When alone, start the horror film fest. If you tie
him to a chair, make sure not to leave any marks. You
could creep up behind him while wearing a mask and
carrying a big knife when he's asleep. Kids love that.

💣 💣 💣 **MISCHIEF** 💣 💣 💣

The Cantering Caterer

....

You will need: a party that you don't want anyone to attend

....

Of course, we all need to throw parties and celebrate from time to time, but sometimes we get roped into it when we wish we hadn't. To get the best of both worlds—kudos from saying yes without the pain of saying yes—tell everyone the party is to feature primarily horse meat—a delicacy in some areas of the world but especially helpful as you live near a racetrack. The party will have no takers.

🕭 🕸 🕭 🕸 **MISCHIEF** 🕭 🕸 🕭 🕸

Make Repellent Coffee

You will need: to have lost your sense of taste and smell

It isn't so hard to make really great coffee; what's really difficult is to make awful coffee that you can claim is chic and an acquired taste. Buy a few cans of the cheapest coffee you can find and mix it all together. Stick it in the oven for an hour or so, then take it out. If it smells awful, it is ready. Serve to coworkers.

Make People Chew Correctly

You will need: high standards of politeness

Pose a theory at lunch that every person is as they chew.
Point out that elegant and successful men chew quietly
but effectively. Dainty women take small bites and
swallow lightly. Your boss has a style of eating, however,
that makes wolfing dogs look demure. Watch everyone
chew self-consciously and laugh.

Have Fun at the Eye Doctor's

· ·

You will need: a timid optometrist

Some eye doctors take too darned long fiddling around your face and getting everything right. Heck, they're only eyes. And you have two, generally. So, in the middle of an eye chart test, start reading words—or ask his opinion, "Do you think that line is clearer in the red or the green? No, tell me the truth!" Puff air into his eyes for a change. Lick his hand if he gets too close.

❦ ❦ ❦ **MISCHIEF** ❦ ❦ ❦

Let Off a Bunch of Fireworks

·······················

You will need: a viable British accent

·······················

The British have a unique holiday involving fireworks, bonfires, and burning effigies, and why should they have all the fun? Build a pile of wood into a bonfire in a park, stuff some old clothes in a human shape, and put it on top. Set flaming rockets off as the sun goes down and light the bonfire. When the police arrive put on a fake accent and tell them that you're celebrating the ancient British holiday of Guy Fawkes.

🔥 🔥 🔥 **MISCHIEF** 🔥 🔥 🔥

Be Understood Abroad

·······················

You will need: a batch of old notes and a cab

·······················

Take out worthless francs, marks, and pesos from teenage trips abroad. While traveling with the cabbie, riffle through notes as though about to bestow billions of dollars on the unsuspecting sap. He will get you to your destination in double-quick time in order to get his hands on all that unusable, pre-euro paper money.

🏴 🕷 🏴 MISCHIEF 🏴 🕷 🏴

Have a Free Vacation

· ·

You will need: a lot of luck

· ·

At the airport, ask a cabbie to wait. Find a limo driver inside who is holding a card with a name on it. Tell him he's wanted at security, and offer to hold his card. When the client arrives, apologize for the car, and take him to the cab. En route, explain you are his guide. Get everything at the hotel charged to him, including your suite, meals, and drinks. Take him to clubs and restaurants. Later, if you want, marry him.

☙ ☙ ☙ **MISCHIEF** ☙ ☙ ☙

Be a New Nurse Nightingale

You will need: some swill or gruel

At this time of year there's always someone who's sick but who insists on going to work. Good thing you were born to help. Make a gruel for them by mixing oats with clean water. Pour into a flask, take to the office, and serve. Alternatively, heat up water, pour it on cardboard, mash, and then serve to the sick person.

●●● OFFICE ●●●

Win an Election

You will need: a sign saying, "Let Me Buy Your Vote"

Tell everyone that the new boss is going to be voted in and offer one dollar for every vote you can get. Ask them to write you onto the ballot. Have the people take a photograph of their voting card and show it to you before you give them their dollar. Get into the office and become a despot. Now, there's a good turnaround for those who take their voting rights too lightly!

● ● ● OFFICE ● ● ●

DEPRESS EVERYONE AT A READING GROUP

. . . .

You will need: some very poor poetry

. . . .

Reading groups are places where people can share feelings and thoughts that reading often stirs up. Find a reading group and read them your own poem—attributed to someone else, naturally—called "Time to Die, Mrs. Nature" and "Oh I Loved That Pig Now Bacon." Remember: it doesn't have to be good, just way too emotional.

✾ ✾ ✾ ETIQUETTE ✾ ✾ ✾

GIVE THE HUMAN TOUCH

....

You will need: very sweaty palms

....

When meeting someone you dislike, shake their hand and then, as if absentmindedly, keep holding onto it. This is best if your palms are dripping with sweat. Hold their hands until they pull away or try to say something about it. Then hold tighter. Pretend not to notice. Act as if they are not attached to you. Continue.

❀ ❀ ❀ ETIQUETTE ❀ ❀ ❀

Get an Upgrade

. . . .

You will need: red eyes and a face that was born to cry

. . . .

Hobble toward the check-in smiling, and say, "Has my husband checked in yet?" When they say they have no idea, burst into tears and say you only bought economy seats because he has gone bankrupt. Start to sob alarmingly while daubing your nose with an incredibly fashionable handkerchief. "And now he's left me." First class, madam?

✸✸✸ LEISURE ✸✸✸

Make Drunk Look Pretty

. . . .

You will need: a lot to drink, waterproof mascara, and the ability to shut up while inebriated

. . . .

"Drunk ugly" is a loaded, obnoxious babe. "Drunk pretty" is when your makeup stays on while you drink and you don't start hog-calling at the top of your lungs. Train yourself to be dainty and sweet even when the room is spinning. If you feel perky, fight that feeling. And get great waterproof mascara (with remover—you'll need that by morning).

✸ ✸ ✸ LEISURE ✸ ✸ ✸

Dump a Date

....

You will need: cab fare home and low heels

....

There's never a bad reason to dump a date. In fact, you will
need all your wiles to make sure your bad date doesn't try
to HELP you in what you are about to do. Figure out what
will turn him off permanently—nosebleed, talk of
becoming a nun, liking Phil Collins—and run with that.
Watch his face drop as he realizes he is not getting sex
from you, ever. Thank him for his time, leave, and get a
cab. Use your flats to run away if necessary.

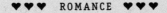

♥♥♥ ROMANCE ♥♥♥

Ruin Autumn

....

You will need: a bunch of really nasty
fallen leaves

....

Only a hard-hearted person would refuse an invitation to
take a walk in the fallen leaves, even if he is your ex and
you had a very nasty breakup. It is better to extend that
olive branch and forget differences in this time of thanks.
So take your ex for a stroll "kickin' leaves and makin' a
leaf wall." Hide cinder blocks in the leaves where he's
kicking. When he falls over in agony, cover him in wet
leaves that maybe a dog has been at and sit on him.
Whistle a happy tune. Give thanks.

❤ ❤ ❤   ROMANCE   ❤ ❤ ❤

GET OUT OF ATTENDING FAMILY GET-TOGETHERS

....

You will need: a smiling face

....

When at the house of your parents or siblings for a family get-together, take tiny bits of all the food and critique it harshly. Use your loudest voice and put a lot of treble in it so it carries. "This must be dog food!" exclaim after tasting the pâté, and "Sparkling wine from Tennessee, who knew?" about the champagne. Smile nicely.

Next year it'll be a restaurant.

☺ ☻ ☹ FAMILY ☺ ☻ ☹

GET GRANNY'S JEWELS NOW

. . . .

You will need: a piece of illegible legal paper and a pal

. . . .

Granny has a bundle of old necklaces, earrings, and bracelets that will, one day, be yours. Why not today? Dash to Granny's house with your friend and arrive out of breath, waving the piece of paper in Gran's face. Tell her that a law is about to be introduced that will ensure that all family heirlooms, particularly jewels, will be taxed at 70% when handed down the line. Get her to sign over all her stuff to you, date and time it, and get your pal to "witness" it.

☺ ☺ ☹ FAMILY ☺ ☺ ☹

Go Back to Work

You will need: a weird smile

After your various brilliant wheezes at work, your coworkers will see you in a whole new light. Most of them will be scared of you. Those that aren't you should be scared of. Make the most of your coworkers' fear by asking them for irrational things—$100, keys to their car, a bite of their lunch. No one will refuse you and no one will do anything about getting them back in case you stab yourself again. Or worse, them.

Invent Your Own Weird Holiday

You will need: a slug on a string

Weird holidays make us aware of things we may not know about. Weird holidays also bring new thoughts into our minds, making us consider life differently. So introduce your coworkers to Slug Day. Go into work and say, "Hey, Slug Day! Let's ooze!" Then lie on the floor and wriggle very slowly toward your seat. Explain that it is both pertinent and proper to bring in an actual slug and hang it around a squeamish girl's neck.

▸▸▸ OFFICE ◂◂◂

Fake Washing Instructions

· ·

You will need: to sew in a label

· ·

There's nothing more annoying than your sister demanding you return an expensive item of clothing that she "lent" you last year. Well, even if you don't care for it anymore, you can still prevent her from enjoying it. Sew inappropriate washing instructions into it: "Use hot water. Always tumble dry."

☺ ☺ ☹ FAMILY ☺ ☺ ☹

Make Over Mother

. . . .

You will need: clothes that hate you

. . . .

Mother's wardrobe needs an overhaul.
Take her shopping and make her buy tight knee
skirts that prevent her from walking very fast. Buy
her linen so she has to always stand and never sit.
Investigate the plethora of catsuit designs that will
stop her from doing much of anything outside
of maybe working on engines.

☺ ☺ ☹ FAMILY ☺ ☺ ☹

Be Special

....

You will need: a whole flotilla of fake allergic reactions

....

Are there some things you really hate? The wise among us develop allergic reactions to things we really cannot stand. The secret? Be consistent. If you don't want red wine at a wedding, hold out for champagne but don't drink red wine afterward. Hate certain foods? Be sure you hate them enough not to eat them even if you are stranded on a mountaintop.

🖤 🖤 🖤 MISCHIEF 🖤 🖤 🖤

Attack a Beauty Counter

....

**You will need: a beauty counter that annoys
you on a regular basis**

....

Go to the beauty counter that you love to hate. Gird your
loins to make mischief. Instead of having them smear you
with lipstick and scent, make them put it on themselves.
Look hard at their skin and make assumptions about their
personal life ("Ah, you've been out late, you little
scamp!"). Insist that they show you all the colors
they sell but wear them on their own faces.

Get to Your Man's Heart via Soup

....

You will need: a resealable carton for liquids

....

Even though it is an arduous process, make your famous broccoli and sauerkraut soup. Place into carton ready to be frozen or stored but label the carton with stickers that read "Do not open here" all over the carton. Deliver to boyfriend with a wan smile and then leave.

♥♥♥ ROMANCE ♥♥♥

Ruin His Brunch (and Psyche)

....

You will need: a lot of food, bulletproof
windows, and a quiet place to stand

....

Ask any man whom you enjoy tormenting to brunch. It's
more fun if he is actually your current boyfriend, but he
could be your boyfriend's best pal. Then invite the
relatives of all his ex-girlfriends. As the aunts of That Slut,
the cousins of The Whiner, and the siblings of Greedy Bitch
meet, they will turn on the man their niece/cousin/sister
once loved and now hate and wreck his psyche to the point
where he can't lift a fork.

♥♥♥ ROMANCE ♥♥♥

Day 331

DESTROY A FAMILY

....

You will need: access to a hamster

....

Remove children's pet hamster from cage and hide in safe place. Lift up rug. Insert wadded tissue full of potato chips and fruitcake. Alert children to absence of pet. When children weepily alert parent to absence of pet, watch as parent treads on lump under rug. As children hear crunch and scream, produce hamster from "behind the sofa where Daddy should have looked in the first place." Imply Mommy is a bad mommy because she has hidden food under the rug, of all places.

☺ ☺ ☹ FAMILY ☺ ☺ ☹

Day 332

BE THE FAMILY ANGEL

....

You will need: a sneaky plan and some nice cookies

....

Extend a bridge of peace to any sibling with whom you have a particularly heated rivalry. Send them a nice e-mail or flowers, or meet up for lunch. Be submissive and gain their trust. Weasel important information out of them and record it for future use (voice recording is good—wear a wire). Not only are you making them feel at ease, you are getting vital information that can be used against them.

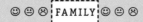 ☺ ☺ ☹ FAMILY ☺ ☺ ☹

MOVE TO BRAZIL

....

You will need: lots of someone else's money

....

If you really, truly, genuinely never want to see a friend again, don't entertain the thought of ending their life, either by accident or on purpose. Merely encourage that friend to lend a significant to mildly more substantial amount of money to you. It is guaranteed that you will never ever see that friend again once you've moved to Brazil.

❋ ❋ ❋ ETIQUETTE ❋ ❋ ❋

MEND A BRIDGE, THEN BURN IT

. . . .

You will need: five old friends you've
fallen out with

. . . .

Invite them all to a meal at a swanky restaurant
on the pretext of patching things up. Arrive last
and demand to know what they've all been
saying about you and that this is a clear-the-air
meeting where anything can be said. Make up
things that one ex-pal said about another. Bitch
like crazy, eat well, and be the first to leave.
Let them pay the bill.

❀ ❀ ❀ ETIQUETTE ❀ ❀ ❀

GET A FREE HAIRCUT

. . . .

You will need: a really good haircutter who is
also extremely sensitive

. . . .

Go to the best hairdresser you know. As she is cutting
your hair, flinch with every movement of her hand as if
you can feel every hair being cut. Tell her you can't
stand the salon's music. Finally, burst into tears when
she shows you her hard, creative work. You won't be
able to return, but you will have the most beautiful free
haircut in the history of hairkind.

☼ ☼ ☼ LEISURE ☼ ☼ ☼

SAVE THE TREES

· ·

You will need: a leafleting campaign

· ·

Leaflet the entire local area, proclaiming "the coming revenge of the trees." "The trees are angry," you write, "so they'll resist being put up in your front room. They'll poke you in the eye, drip sap, catch fire, and be impossible to clean up after they dry out. To show their lasting anger you will find their needles wedged in your carpet even in the summer months." Buy a stock of artificial trees and sell on the street corner.

☼☼☼ LEISURE ☼☼☼

Honor Your Coworkers

You will need: a free hour or so

You're so popular that of course your coworkers invite you out after work all the time (and if they don't, it's because they're in awe of you, so invite yourself). But you have to let everyone know that you are coming ONLY if there is something nice involved—an expensive goody bag for you or a chair next to a hunky guy. You should also let everyone know that bad things will happen if you don't get your way. Some people could lose their jobs—or their hair.

Be the Competition

You will need: access to someone else's
e-mail account

Use a rival's computer to send unfunny comedy e-mails
around the office—if you're feeling really bad, send
pornographic attachments or even viruses. You could
send photos of kittens, yummy food, and ponies. Attach
hard-to-resist game programs.

N.B. Make sure your office doesn't have CCTV.

Day 339

MAKE MEANINGFUL FAMILY COOKIES

You will need: large cookie cutters and a pastry bag

For your next family get-together, make a batch of "tattletale family secret" cookies. Spread the baked cookies with frosting, and using the pastry bag, write things on the cookies like, "Billy stole money from Mom's purse," "Dad kept a bottle of Jack Daniel's under the bed," or "Mom made Granny change the will."

☺ ☺ ☹ FAMILY ☺ ☺ ☹

BOOK A FAMILY VACATION

You will need: access to the Internet and a parent's credit card

Isn't it about time that the whole family gathered together at some exotic location—or at least out of state? Surprise your parents by sneaking one of their credit cards away from them and booking a house somewhere a long ways away. Invite all your siblings and their families, but make sure that it's a surprise for Mom and Pop. Oh, and then pretend you can't make it. Stay at their house for the duration.

☺ ☺ ☹ FAMILY ☺ ☺ ☹

Be Once, Twice, Three Times a Lady

. . . .

You will need: to do nothing

. . . .

Everyone longs for those golden days of yore when women were ladies and men knew their place—serving them. Today you will bring a little bit of the good old days back into your life. Wear a large dress with lots of petticoats and a bonnet of some sort. Do not open a door; wait until a gentleman does it. Don't sit down until a chair is pulled out for you. And do not pay for anything.

❀ ❀ ❀ ETIQUETTE ❀ ❀ ❀

Get Totally Wired as Insurance

....

You will need: to wear a wire

....

It's not that you can't handle your drink—it's just that, being who you are, you are more likely to get into scrapes than the wallflower who can't even mix a drink. Wearing an FBI-style wire will record all that is uttered by you and those around you at any kind of social gathering where alcohol is taken—and you don't have to use it as evidence the next day if you don't want to.

❀ ❀ ❀ ETIQUETTE ❀ ❀ ❀

Help Out an Old Friend

....

You will need: a friend's trust

....

Ask a friend if you can help to stage a special meal for her and her boyfriend. Buy all of the ingredients needed for a difficult-to-make but delicious meal for two and offer to help her make it. Turn up half an hour late to help out, wearing something inappropriate for cooking. Sip wine as she cooks and then stay for dinner (how can they let you leave now?). Chat him up as she sweats in the kitchen. Leave before cleaning up.

❧ ❧ ❧ **MISCHIEF** ❧ ❧ ❧

Put on a Bad Art Show

....

You will need: one pretentious artist friend, a rented gallery, and some crayons and paper

....

Draw any old thing on a piece of paper and have it framed. Repeat until you have enough for your own show. Rent a fashionable art gallery and get some friends to come to the opening night. Invite the pretentious art friend. Have everyone ooh and aah over your drawings; get someone to pretend they are a famous art critic and have them make proclamations. Watch your pretentious friend turn blue.

🔴 🔴 🔴 MISCHIEF 🔴 🔴 🔴

Day 345

GET A PET

....

You will need: living parents

....

Pets are great for your health. Alas, they take a lot of looking after. But if you still have parents, they love looking after living things. Enjoy your pet for a month or so and then dump it on your Mom and Pop. Tell them it's temporary and that you'll have it back in a few weeks. If you've chosen a horse as a pet, ensure that your parents live on a farm, or at least in a two-bedroom apartment with a view.

☺ ☺ ☹ **FAMILY** ☺ ☺ ☹

GIVE GIFTS SPONTANEOUSLY

· ·

You will need: a fast trip to the grocery store, some newspaper, and red ribbon

· ·

Endear yourself to your family by giving them surprise presents at any time. Simply buy some pasta sauce, dried pasta, and preshaved mozzarella; grab a few jars of olives and a few boxes of cookies. You may want to throw in some pudding and cake mixes, "naughty" candies, and some weird food with a label in Urdu. Wrap all these up in newspaper, tied with a red ribbon. Your family will think you're so generous and creative. Little will they know you are cheap and hate them.

 ☺ ☺ ☹ FAMILY ☺ ☺ ☹

Become the iPod Queen

You will need: download capability

Is there anything worse than having to put up with the office bore forever crowing about their iPod and their stupid playlists? Offer to turn them on to something truly great; drop hints about how cool this one site is that only you know about. When office bore is hooked and longing to know what the site is, borrow their MP3 player and "accidentally" wipe everything that's on there, replacing it with as many tracks as possible from any number of Muzak download sites.

➤➤➤ OFFICE ➤➤➤

Make $200 with Minimal Effort

You will need: a $200 item of clothing that is long and skinny

First, borrow a very expensive scarf. Wear said scarf to the office. When asked to shred documents at the office, dip the scarf into the shredder with one finger on the off button. Stop shredder after half the scarf is wrecked and scream loudly. The company will reimburse you the $200 for the scarf.

●●● OFFICE ●●●

PLAN YOUR OWN FUNERAL

....

You will need: a little black dress

....

You've lived your life in style, so you'll want to go out with equal dash and élan. Visit undertakers in a little black dress. Tell them the funeral is for you and they'll give you a great deal. And they'll look so cute and surprised when you tell them the ceremony will be in 50 years or so. Oh, and you can demand certain songs, too—"Diamonds Are a Girl's Best Friend" should be on the list, of course.

❀ ❀ ❀ ETIQUETTE ❀ ❀ ❀

REALLY ENJOY
A PARTY

....

You will need: a really horrible bottle
of wine and one gorgeous bottle, both
hidden in your bag

....

Bring a good bottle to a riotous party and you'll

not see it again until it's empty. So, bring a bottle

of something that really should be eating through

the glass bottle. Let that be imbibed by the masses.

Meanwhile, pull the good one from your bag and

drink it all on your own. If the host catches you,

offer a slurp but no more.

❀ ❀ ❀   ETIQUETTE   ❀ ❀ ❀

Come to Terms with Mortality

....

You will need: elderly relatives

....

After planning your funeral, your thoughts will turn to mortality. Call that rich elderly relative and let them know that you're thinking of them and looking forward to seeing more of them next year. It'll earn you Brownie points and maybe even a bit more of the estate.

☺ ☺ ☹ FAMILY ☺ ☺ ☹

Leave Your Mark

....

You will need: a gift voucher for a tattoo parlor

....

Make sure that your nephew or niece will always remember you by slipping them a gift voucher for a tattoo parlor downtown. Arrange with the tattooist beforehand that whatever the kids want, they get a heart with "Auntie" entwined with barbed wire instead. When their parents protest, exclaim your innocence.

☺ ☺ ☹ FAMILY ☺ ☺ ☹

Throw an Impromptu Office Party

You will need: photos of last year's party

Arrive with bottles of vodka, and lots of colorful glossy photos from last year's party, showing just how incredibly stupid everyone looked. Tell the newcomers who those strange faces in the photos are (the people who lost their jobs after the party). Use your talents with Photoshop to make the photos seem scarier and worse than they really are. Crack open the bottles at lunchtime and suggest a game of Spin the Bottle.

Be Pregnant
for the Day

You will need: to keep a straight face

As soon as you arrive at work, dash to the toilet and make puking sounds in a stall. Creep your way gently to your seat and then burst into tears. Let only one person know that you think you're pregnant. Soon everyone will know and they'll be so nice to you all day. Just before the end of the day, go to the bathroom and come out smiling, saying "Phew, it's okay. False alarm." Get taken out for a celebratory dinner by your coworkers!

●●● OFFICE ●●●

Act Married

....

You will need: a ring on your left hand

....

There's nothing more predatory than a single woman at a social gathering, especially a dinner party. Wives hate you. Men want you. Single guys fear you. The hostess smiles at you. Your coat disappears. So act married. Act graceful, demure, and not needy. This is the only way you'll attract a man, and you only want a one-night stand anyway, right?

❀ ❀ ❀ ETIQUETTE ❀ ❀ ❀

Create the Best Round-Robin

. . . .

You will need: the gall to send the same
letter out to all the people you know

. . . .

Mention a few people whom no one knows—"Then a dark
figure appeared and before I could speak, I fainted!" Add a
well-known person—"But luckily, before I hit the ground,
Tom Cruise came and saved me!" Put in a bit about
yourself—"I learned how to run the toaster, so that was
good," and then a bit about your hopes for the future.
Expect far less contact with the recipients of your Round-
Robin letter from now on.

❀ ❀ ❀ ETIQUETTE ❀ ❀ ❀

Be a Vamp

You will need: a full-length mirror and no taste

It's so dull wearing boring old office clothes at work, so enter work today in style—show a little cleavage, a bit of leg, and let your hair down. Paint your face white with slabs of black mascara and scarlet lipstick. Back comb your hair and smoke Russian cigarettes in a long holder. Whenever anyone comes near you say, "I vant to be alone." Have a good time scaring everyone.

➤ ➤ ➤ **OFFICE** ➤ ➤ ➤

Play a Drinking Game at Lunch

You will need: a double-headed coin

Drinking makes lunchtime more fun—there are no more awkward silences, no more diplomatic hesitations. Make today's lunch a memorable event by saying to yourself, "I will drink a cocktail if it's heads and not if it's tails." Toss your coin at least six times. Later, use the coin to figure out which is your coat and then, even later, which floor you're on, and which blurry person may be your boss.

● ● ● OFFICE ● ● ●

Create Suspicion

· ·

You will need: your boss's home number

Enter the home telephone number of your boss on your
frequent caller list. Make sure that caller ID is switched
off on your phone. Call after 9 p.m. when the kids are
in bed and there's a good chance that his wife will
answer. When she does, "stifle" a gasp, hold the phone
close, breathe, and say nothing for 30 seconds before
hanging up. Repeat over the course of a week.

🖤 🖤 🖤 MISCHIEF 🖤 🖤 🖤

Consider a Career Change

....

You will need: to feign interest

A change is as good as a rest (apparently), and variety is
the spice of life—so consider a radical change of career.
Why not try police work? (And if you are already a
police officer, you really shouldn't be reading this
book.) Find an officer and engage him—won't work on a
her—in conversation about your becoming an officer.
After as long as you can take it say, "Sorry, maybe an IT
analyst would be more interesting," and walk away.

🔥 🔥 🔥 MISCHIEF 🔥 🔥 🔥

Surprise an Ex-Lover

. . . .

You will need: a friend who is almost a professional you-know-what

. . . .

Find out where your ex-boyfriend (any will do) is going to be tonight and arrange to be there. Take a friend with you who is so forward and dresses so outrageously that drag queens envy her. Tell her that "that man over there" (your ex) just loves to be hugged and kissed and touched in public, that he loves to be hung all over. Set her off on her way. (And hope that he doesn't really love it.)

☼ ☼ ☼ LEISURE ☼ ☼ ☼

Return "Gifts" Properly

. . . .

You will need: a believable smile

. . . .

Gather all the items of clothing that you bought in the last six months but are bored with. Set about returning them to various stores with a sad tale about how your sister wore it once before she was tragically killed in an accident. Never mind the receipts— everyone will be too embarrassed to question whether the stuff was bought at their store. You might even get money back.

☼ ☼ ☼ LEISURE ☼ ☼ ☼

Gate-Crash a Wake

. . . .

You will need: indoor fireworks

. . . .

The local newspaper will have details of any wakes, or "memorial services," being held in your area. Choose the swankiest-sounding one and turn up wearing something black and just below the knee. Wait until after the speeches and the food has gone around and then let off a few indoor fireworks. That ought to lighten things up a bit. Start "Aaaah"-ing as each one bursts into flame. Tell everyone it's what the deceased would have wanted.

❀ ❀ ❀ ETIQUETTE ❀ ❀ ❀

Make a Baby Excuse

....

You will need: a baby

....

Need to leave a social gathering early? Nothing makes you want to leave earlier—or have people want you to leave early—than to bring a baby to anywhere that adults smoke, drink, and get outrageous. Walk around with the baby in your arms tutting and shaking your head for a bit first, though. Just to make sure everyone feels guilty without knowing why.

❀ ❀ ❀ ETIQUETTE ❀ ❀ ❀

Dump Your Boyfriend and Enjoy a One-Night Stand

. . . .

You will need: a face mask in your handbag

. . . .

Ditch the boyfriend at 11 p.m. Start an argument at a party and pour a sticky cocktail over his head. March off. Find a guy that you like, put on your mask, and start kissing him at 11:55 p.m. Do not give him your real name. Go to his place or a motel. Turn off your cell phone.

(Go back to Day 1 for what to do next.)

❤ ❤ ❤   ROMANCE   ❤ ❤ ❤

Acknowledgments

In the way of acknowledgments, gratitude
first goes to Mal Peachey, my fearless leader
and sensible luncheon adviser, for showing me
there was more bad advice in me than I had
previously thought. The book would not exist
without him. Thank you also to my mother,
Eve Finley, a true paragon of naughtiness and a
genius at bad advice (despite my father John's
more moral nature). Thanks, too, to my husband,
David Quantick, for letting me throw out ideas to
his nimble mind. Finally, a most enormous thank-
you to Dmitri Bilgere, who brainstormed the best
bits of this book with me (and, yes, most of it did
actually happen). This slim tome commemorates
the times we'd shop at the Willy St. Co-op
in Madison, Wisconsin, just to torment
anyone there. I'm mighty grateful.

Karen Krizanovich

Bad Things

To Do